D1565417

A CHRISTIAN GUIDE
TO PROSPERITY

By Michael Fries and C. Holland Taylor

with Ron Sunseri

Illustrated by Keith Jefferds

COMMUNICATIONS RESEARCH
OAKLAND, CALIFORNIA

Communications Research
P.O. Box 11143
Oakland, CA 94611

Designed by Barry Geller.

Grateful acknowledgement is made of the following for permission to reprint previously published and copyrighted material:

Excerpt from *The Law* by Frederic Bastiat. Translated from the French by Dean
Russell. Copyright © 1950. (Irvington-on-Hudson, New York: Foundation for Economic Education), p. 21. All rights reserved.

Excerpt from *For a New Liberty* by Murray N. Rothbard. Copyright © 1973. (New
York: Macmillan), pp. 178-182. All rights reserved.

Library of Congress Cataloging in Publication Data

Fries, Michael, 1938–
    A Christian guide to prosperity.

    Bibliography: p.
    1. Finance, Personal. 2. Success. 3. Industry and state—United States. 4. United
States—Economic policy—1981–   . I. Taylor, C. Holland. II. Sunseri, Ron. III. Title.
HG179.F736   1984   332.024'2   83-46178
ISBN 0-9611910-5-8

He who gives heed to the Word will prosper, and happy is he who trusts in the Lord.

PROVERBS 16:20

CONTENTS

Part I

1. The Richest Man in the World 1
2. "I Promise" 71
3. The Truth about Inflation 121
4. Gambling 161
5. We, the People 177
6. The Party is Over 209
7. The Three Paths 241

Part II

8. Protecting Yourself in the Years to Come 287
9. Gold 311
10. Antiques, Gems, and Real Estate 349
11. Deflation-Proofing Your Investments 369
12. Gaining Control of Your Life 397
13. Changing Yourself 447
14. Changing the Nation 485

Appendix 511
Recommended Reading 519

PART ONE

1

THE RICHEST MAN
IN THE WORLD

We have something that you want.

You do? What is it?

It's something everyone wants, but few people have. It is called

KNOWLEDGE.[1]

What do you mean, knowledge? Knowledge of what?

KNOWLEDGE OF HOW TO GET WHAT
YOU WANT OUT OF LIFE.[2]

Is this a joke? Are you telling me you can actually put money in my pocket?

Do you want more money?

That's not all I want.

What else, then?

When I go shopping, I want my money to buy more. Prices are much too high. And when I get paid, I want to keep more of my money. I'm willing to pay my fair share of taxes, but taxes today are ridiculous.

Is there anything else that you want?

Yes. I'm thinking of buying a bigger house, and my wife needs a new car. I think interest rates should stay at a reasonable level so we can afford these things. I'm also worried about my job. My employer says that if interest rates were lower, I could get a raise. But as things stand now, our company could go out of business.

Are you saying you can solve these problems for me?

We can show you how to solve them *yourself*.

How can I possibly do that? High taxes, inflation, and interest rates are beyond my control. All I know is that something has to change.

Perhaps we can point out a few things you should know.

What do you have in mind?

In order to get what you want out of life, you need to understand what is happening in our economy and how it affects you. You need to understand the realities facing us today.

What realities are you talking about?

You may not know it, but something is coming toward you.

There is?

Yes, and if you don't act quickly, you may be hurt.

Hurt? By what?

By . . .

RAPID ECONOMIC CHANGE.

What are you talking about?

For one thing, the rate of inflation could increase dramatically.

Unemployment could also get worse in the years ahead.

There could even be a breakdown in the social order.

We're not saying a crisis is inevitable, but a tidal wave of rapid change *is* approaching. You should recognize the danger and prepare to meet it.

Imagine you lived in New York City and one morning heard news that a tidal wave was two hundred miles from shore. You would not know for sure that it was going to hit your apartment, but you would want to take steps to protect yourself. It would be foolish to plug your ears and pretend there was no danger.

Even if you're right, what can I do? I'm just one person. I don't have any influence or power.

There are steps you can take to protect yourself, regardless of what happens in the economy. There are also things you can do to help prevent a catastrophe from occurring. But first, it is important that you understand what the problems are.

I'm a busy man. Why do I have to deal with this? Can't the government take care of these problems for me?

Many of our problems have been *caused* by government.

But wouldn't the government do something to prevent a depression?

It could try, by printing and spending a lot of money to keep factories open and workers employed. But that would only postpone a depression and make it worse in the long run. You see, policies like these have nearly destroyed our economy and have led us to the point where we are now—facing one of the greatest dangers of our generation. If we let things continue as they have for the past fifty years, even more serious problems are inevitable.

How do I know you're not just trying to scare me? People have been shouting about a crisis for the past ten years, but I don't have any way of knowing if what they say is true. I don't know anything about economics.

Then let us give you the facts so you can decide for yourself.

Now you're making sense. What are the facts?

First of all, many people are short of cash. As a result, they are forced to buy less, which lowers their standard of living. Our standard of living is falling in America today and will continue to fall until we take corrective steps.

I can see that.

Also, inflation has been getting more serious over the years.

I don't know about that. Prices have been going up as long as I can remember. Why can't inflation continue another fifty years without getting out of hand?

Prices rise slowly at the beginning of any inflation. Then they rise faster and faster until one of two things happens. Either the government stops increasing the money supply—halting inflation in its tracks—or the government continues inflating until the currency of the nation becomes worthless.[3]

18

Could that ever happen in America?

Yes, it could. It happened during the Revolutionary War, and it has happened in many other countries around the world—Germany, France, Hungary, and China, to name a few. Unfortunately, the process is now in motion once again.

Inflation moves up and down, in cycles, but each time it rises, it goes higher than it was before.

YEAR

By the first quarter of 1980, inflation had climbed to more than 15% a year—and was threatening to get WAY OUT OF CONTROL. Since then we've had a slight breathing spell—we've been in the downward cycle—but our problems with inflation are by no means over yet.

Whenever the government tries to reduce inflation, it causes a recession —such as the recessions of 1970, 1974-75 and 1981-82. During a recession the inflation rate goes down for a while. But in order to end the recession before too many companies go bankrupt, the Federal Reserve begins increasing the money supply again. Within a year or two, the inflation rate starts climbing once more.

Since 1970 the dollar has lost more than 60% of its purchasing power.

For over twenty years now, people have been losing confidence in the dollar, and their behavior has changed as a result. Instead of saving part of what they earn each month, many people spend their entire paycheck.[4] Then they borrow even more money to buy what they want before prices can rise even higher.

You're right! I do that myself sometimes. Last fall, I bought a new car. Instead of holding off for another year, I thought I'd better go ahead and buy it now since you don't know what the price will be if you wait.

It sounds like you have *inflationary expectations.*

I guess I do.

You're not the only one. Financial markets have become extremely sensitive to the rate of inflation and government debt. If the government weakens in its resolve to beat inflation, there could be a sudden panic, a massive flight from the dollar, and a world-wide monetary collapse.

I think you're using scare tactics again.

No, we are just telling you the truth. But let's put the question of inflation aside for a moment. It's only one of many factors contributing to our present crisis.

What are some of the others?

The huge amount of public and private debt we have in America.[5]

Also, the threat of many businesses going bankrupt, causing unemployment to reach a massive scale.

Couldn't the government prevent that from happening?

As we said before, it could try. But thousands of companies in America, including some of the largest, are losing money year after year. The government is powerful—powerful enough to save Lockheed and Chrysler if it wants—but it is not powerful enough to save all these companies if they go bankrupt. If a number of key industries fail, and millions of workers are thrown out of their jobs . . .

Stop! That can't happen. We can't have another depression. There must be *someone* who will save us!

The fire department is powerful. It can put out almost any fire. But when a whole city is burning, the situation is beyond their control.

Then God will save us!

There is an old saying we need to remember now: God will bless those who follow His principles.

Now it shall be, if you will diligently obey the Lord your God, being careful to do all His commandments which I command you today, the Lord your God will set you high above all the nations of the earth.

And all these blessings shall come upon you and overtake you, if you will obey the Lord your God.

Blessed shall you be in the city, and blessed shall you be in the country.

Blessed shall be the offspring of your body and the produce of your ground and the offspring of your beasts, the increase of your herd and the young of your flock.

Blessed shall be your basket and your kneading bowl.

Blessed shall you be when you come in, and blessed shall you be when you go out.

The Lord will cause your enemies who rise up against you to be defeated before you; they shall come out against you one way and shall flee before you seven ways.

The Lord will command the blessing upon you in your barns and in all that you put your hand to, and He will bless you in the land which the Lord your God gives you.

The Lord will establish you as a holy people to Himself, as He swore to you, if you will keep the commandments of the Lord your God and walk in His ways.

So all the peoples of the earth shall see that you are called by the name of the Lord: and they shall be afraid of you.

And the Lord will make you abound in prosperity, in the offspring of your body and in the offspring of your beast and in the produce of your ground, in the land which the Lord swore to your fathers to give to you. The Lord will open for you His good storehouse, the heavens, to give rain to your land in its season and to bless all the work of your hand.

DEUTERONOMY 28:1–14.

This is why we are talking with you. We want to show how you can help yourself and your country overcome the dangers we are facing.

But what can I do?

The first thing you need to do is to understand what the problem is.

The situation seems so complex. How will I ever understand it?[6]

Actually, the issues are easy to understand if they are presented in a straightforward way. However, before we explain anything, we would like to tell you a little story.

That's great! I love stories.

This is the story of the Richest Man in the World—a man so rich that everyone knew of his wealth and power. He owned a prosperous business, run by millions of employees, and his income was huge. In fact, his reputation was so great that whenever he wanted to borrow money, people lined up and practically begged for the opportunity to lend it to him.

One year a man named Jim, who had lent the Rich Man a lot of money, decided to travel around the world.

In his travels, Jim was shocked to learn that in every country in the world, there were people who had lent the Rich Man money.

At first he couldn't believe that the Rich Man had borrowed so much
money.

When he realized he was only one of thousands of creditors, Jim became frightened. "Even if he *is* the Richest Man in the World," he thought, "I don't see how he can possibly pay back all these loans. I think I'd better cash in my IOU's now, before it's too late."

Jim cabled home immediately to ask for repayment of his loan. The next day he received a message saying that the Rich Man had broken his promise to repay his debts in gold. Because his IOU's had always been fully backed by gold, they were respected throughout the world. But now the Rich Man was only giving pieces of paper to his creditors as payment for his debt.

Of course, his creditors protested. But the Rich Man replied that they were going to have to accept the paper because he could not afford to repay his debt in gold.

Jim was outraged and began to talk with other people, cautiously at first. Soon he realized they too saw what was happening and were also trying to get rid of the Rich Man's IOU's.

None of these people trusted him to repay the full amount of his loans. Many creditors decided to sell his IOU's for IOU's issued by more responsible businessmen. Others exchanged them for silver or gold, which caused the price of precious metals to rise higher and higher.

Still, for a long time, few people were aware of the Rich Man's huge mountain of debt. Even fewer doubted his intention, or ability, to repay them. After all, he was the Richest Man in the World.

As time passed, however, it became apparent that instead of spending less and paying off his loans, the Richest Man in the World was borrowing even *larger* amounts of money. Eventually, it got to the point where he was borrowing billions of dollars each week, and everyone knew it. This caused interest rates to rise, since the Rich Man was competing with everyone else for all the available money.

Serious problems developed almost immediately. Many people found they could no longer borrow money at reasonable rates of interest. Many people and businesses went bankrupt because of this situation.

People began to question whether anyone—even the Richest Man in the World—could afford to repay so much money. They wondered what he was spending his money on, and whether he could cut back on his lifestyle to start paying back his loans. But nobody knew if he would change. They didn't even know if he recognized the problem himself.

Finally, some of the Rich Man's friends asked him if he could cut back on his spending. The Rich Man seemed surprised by their question. "Absolutely not," he said. "I have millions of employees—with their families—depending on me for jobs. I've asked many of them if they could find other work, but they all said no. All they know is their present job. I can't fire them and let them go hungry.

"Besides, my relatives are always asking me for help. They've all come to depend on me. When I ask them to rely on themselves, they all say they need help—even the ones who are making a good living."

When Jim heard this story, he told his friends that he was more worried than ever. "What do we care about the Richest Man in the World?" they replied.

"Don't you understand?" Jim asked. "If he goes bankrupt, everyone will be affected. The Richest Man in the World is now at the mercy of people's confidence. The only reason anyone still lends him money is because they believe he can repay it. But every year he is spending much more than he earns. If that doesn't change soon, he'll go bankrupt, and the people who depend on him for jobs and support will all be out in the cold.

"Besides that, the people who depend on them for business will also be affected. If the Richest Man in the World goes broke, all the people who have lent him money will never be repaid. A wave of bankruptcies could sweep the nation."

What does it mean to go bankrupt?

Bankruptcy means *to die financially*. When you don't have enough money to exist from day to day, you die financially.

By this time, the Rich Man was coming very close to bankruptcy, and he didn't even know he was in danger. Only a thin thread of confidence was keeping him alive, and the people who lent him money were beginning to know it.

Given this situation, a panic could develop overnight. If people suddenly heard that the Rich Man was going bankrupt, there would be a panic to sell his IOU's for *anything* they would bring. The panic would affect everyone, rich and poor alike. Banks would close and thousands of companies would go bankrupt. Millions of people could lose their jobs.

Is that what eventually happens in your story?

We haven't reached the end of our story yet. Let's go on.

As time passed, more and more people realized that they were affected by everything the Rich Man did. Finally, they went to him and told him it would be better to cut back on his spending immediately, rather than going bankrupt and dragging everyone else with him.

At first the Rich Man protested. "My employees and relatives will never allow this," he said.

"Don't they understand what will happen if you don't reduce your spending?" his visitors asked. "You'll go bankrupt, and then you won't be able to help them at all."

"I don't think that has ever occurred to them," the Rich Man replied, "and to tell you the truth, it didn't even occur to me until just now. Almost everyone believes my wealth is unlimited. They've always been told there's nothing the Richest Man in the World can't do, nothing he can't provide. They're going to be shocked to hear otherwise."

"Are you going to tell them?" they asked.

"I don't have any choice," the Rich Man replied. Soon afterwards he called all of his relatives and employees together. He told them that for many years he had been more generous with them than he could afford. Although his business was a prosperous one, the amount of money he had spent on friends, employees, and relatives was more than he had made in years. Now he was saddled with a huge debt, and he could not go on much longer without facing bankruptcy. Therefore, he was compelled to ask everyone to make do with fewer benefits. Some, he said, would even have to find new jobs.

Everyone was stunned. When they realized what the Rich Man was saying and the sacrifice he was asking them to make, people started shaking their heads and shouting, "No, no! We can't do it."

His employees said, "We've been working for you for years. You can't fire us like this. Our jobs are too important!"

His relatives said, "You have to take care of us. You owe it to us."

What happened?

We don't know what happened. The story hasn't ended yet, but there is one thing we can tell you.

What's that?

We can tell you the name of the Richest Man in the World. His name is...

UNCLE SAM!

Uncle Sam! If his name is Uncle Sam, who is everyone else?

The employees in our story are people who work for the government. The Rich Man's relatives are all those Americans—over 130 million by now—who receive government support of one kind or another. Some of these people are:

Homeowners, real estate brokers, construction workers, building suppliers, and mortgage lenders—almost everyone associated with housing. Over $60,000,000,000 in home loans were guaranteed by the government in 1982.

The list of businesses that supply goods and services to the government is almost endless.

Dozens of foreign countries receive low interest loans guaranteed by the United States Government. If these countries default on their loans, the American taxpayer will be stuck with the bill.

Many farmers receive crop subsidies from the government.

Large banks and corporations also benefit from Uncle Sam's generosity. None of these people are poor, but they are still receiving government handouts year after year.

What about all the talk of bankruptcy? What does that mean?

If the federal government goes bankrupt because of its reckless spending, it will affect all of us. We are facing that danger right now, even though most of us don't know it.

Does that mean *I'm* in danger too?

Remember what we said earlier?

What was that?

**YOU MAY NOT KNOW IT,
BUT SOMETHING IS COMING TOWARD YOU!**

Look behind you now. It's almost here.

I'll be crushed. I've got to get out of here!

THIS IS ONE TIME
YOU'RE NOT GOING TO ESCAPE
BY RUNNING AWAY
FROM YOUR PROBLEMS.

Don't underestimate me! I'm a good runner!

We don't doubt it, but this time you're trapped. There's nowhere for you to run or hide.

How did I get into this situation? How on earth did the problem ever get so big?

This is what happens when you run away from your problems year after year. They keep coming after you, growing larger all the time. Finally, you reach a point where you cannot avoid them any longer. This is the situation in America today. We've been afraid to deal with the problems of our economy, so these problems have been growing over the years. Now they're about to crush us—and they will if we don't act soon.

What can I do?

YOU HAVE TO MEET THIS PROBLEM HEAD-ON, AND OVERCOME IT!

Me? Overcome this? Impossible! The problem is much too big.

No, it's not too big. You just think you're smaller than you really are.

Once you understand the basic cause of our economic problems, you will be able to recognize their solution. You will know what steps you should take to protect yourself and your family in the years ahead, and you will be in a better position to help solve the problems which confront our nation as a whole.

But how can I solve these problems if the danger is so great?

A steamroller seems formidable when it is coming straight at you. Yet, it's easy to control if you can get behind the wheel.

There are many currents flowing through society, affecting each of us to one degree or another. One of these currents is sweeping towards crisis, and anyone caught in this stream may be hurt badly in the years to come.

Fortunately, there is another MORE POWERFUL current also moving through our society. This second current is working to produce vast social and technological progress. If you learn to move in this stream, it can take you wherever you want to go. You can protect yourself from rapid change and begin to enjoy the prosperity everyone will experience in the future *right now*.

Are you saying that we will return to a time of prosperity?

Yes, once our economic problems have been solved.

As technology becomes more sophisticated and as people learn to cooperate with one another, a huge amount of wealth will be produced. Then, a more prosperous time will be here for all of us.

If we change government policies, inflation will become a thing of the past. Your money will buy much more than it does today. A decrease in restrictive government regulations will allow businesses to thrive and to pay their employees more. Lower taxes will also mean more money in your pocket. We will all have more money to save, spend, and invest— and a greater incentive to produce.

THE CREATIVE GENIUS OF AMERICA WILL EXPLODE.

Let me ask another question. If this "boom" lies somewhere in the future, how can I make my finances work now?

YOU CAN BECOME
A FORERUNNER OF PROSPERITY
AND ACTUALLY HELP BRING IT ABOUT.

How can I do that?

By getting into shape.

Imagine you are an athlete in training. No one gets in shape in just a day or two. But if you start working now, the payoff will come much sooner than you expect.

What should I do to get in shape?

For one thing, you must prepare yourself financially. A great transition is now underway in America and in the world. Eventually, it will lead to great prosperity for all of us.

However, while some people welcome change and benefit from it, there are always those who resist progress. The next few years will be a time of rapid change. There may be some discomfort—especially if change is resisted by a majority of Americans. You may experience financial hardship in the years ahead unless you take steps to protect yourself now—to shield yourself and your family from any adversity that may come your way. To do that

> YOU MUST GET OUT OF DEBT AND SAVE MONEY.
> YOU MUST ALSO LEARN HOW TO PROTECT THE
> PURCHASING POWER OF YOUR SAVINGS.

When you succeed at this, you will be prepared for the future and enjoy the present much more. You will be protected from the financial hardships which, over the next few years, may strike those who are unprepared for rapid economic change.

I think my finances are already in good shape. I have a good job, a car, and a house that's worth a lot of money.

How much cash do you have?

Not much.

Then you still have something to learn about investments. During a time of rapid change, it is necessary to have more cash on hand than when things are stable.

You also need to develop certain qualities in yourself. Conditions in your environment may shift dramatically from one day to the next. Your bank could fail; you could lose your job; or there might be another oil embargo with a shortage of gasoline and fuel to heat your home.

In order to preserve your sanity in the years to come, you must be flexible. You need the ability to respond quickly and effectively to any challenge without being thrown off balance.

You must be kidding! How do you expect anyone to lose their job without being thrown off balance?

If you know you can find a better job and have enough cash to take care of yourself in the meantime, you can take the loss in stride. There are two ways you can react to losing a job: you can worry and feel sorry for yourself, or you can take practical steps towards finding another way to earn a living.[7] There are plenty of opportunities in America, more now than ever before. But they exist only for those who KNOW WHAT THEY WANT AND HOW TO GET IT.

Knowing where you want to go and understanding why is like having a map which can guide you to your destination, wherever it may be.[8]

This applies to investment decisions and to all decisions which affect the direction of your personal life.

> ONCE YOU RECOGNIZE YOUR MAJOR GOALS IN LIFE, YOU WILL BE WELL ON THE WAY TO CONTROLLING YOUR DESTINY.

How do I know what goals I should set for myself?

That will become apparent during our discussion. You will have to set your own personal and financial goals although we will help you get in touch with what these are.

Before you will feel comfortable taking any of our advice, however, you will want to understand what is happening to the economy, what is causing inflation, and where it may lead. For example, we don't want you to buy gold just because we say so. You should buy gold for the same reason that everyone else who understands the economy is buying it— because gold is a protection against inflation and monetary collapse.

Alright, let's imagine I set certain goals for myself over the next few years. How am I going to achieve them? Not many things are as simple as going out and buying gold. Won't it be hard to get what I want out of life?[9]

Not if you know how to go about it in the right way. In order to be successful, there are certain qualities you must develop in yourself— stability,[10] flexibility, self-confidence,[11] enthusiasm, persistence,[12] and generosity,[13] to name a few. These qualities will help you achieve

COMPLETE PERSONAL AND FINANCIAL INDEPENDENCE.

Success and character go hand in hand. Once you have mastered the laws of success—by developing your character[14]—you will be able to set any reasonable goal for yourself and achieve it quickly.

I'm encouraged by what you say.

I can see myself now, rising above all my problems . . .[15]

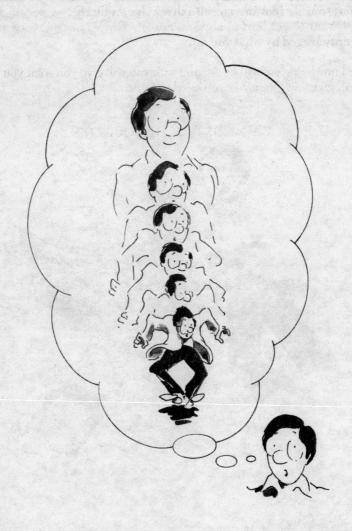

But to be frank with you, and realistic, I'm not ready to tackle the world quite yet. I think you'd better tell me more.

What do you want to know?

I want to know how to cope with the problems that may come my way. I don't want to get buried under a tide of change. I need more control over my life.

The knowledge we will be sharing with you will give you what you want. It will give you the power you need to

GAIN CONTROL OF YOUR LIFE.[16]

NOTES

1. Hosea 4:6. My people are destroyed for the lack of knowledge.

2. Proverbs 11:9. Through knowledge the righteous will be delivered.

3. Proverbs 20:10. Differing weights and differing measures, both of them are abominable to the Lord.

4. Proverbs 13:22. A good man leaves an inheritance to his children's children.

5. Proverbs 22:7. The rich rules over the poor, and the borrower becomes the lender's slave.

6. Proverbs 2:1–7. My son, if you will receive my sayings, and treasure my commandments within you,

   Make your ear attentive to wisdom, incline your heart to understanding;

   For if you cry for discernment, lift your voice for understanding;

   If you seek her as silver, and search for her as for hidden treasures;

   Then you will discern the fear of the Lord, and discover the knowledge of God.

   For the Lord gives wisdom; from His mouth come knowledge and understanding.

   He stores up sound wisdom for the upright; He is a shield to those who walk in integrity.

7. Psalms 37:23. The steps of a man are established by the Lord; and He delights in his way.

8. Proverbs 29:18. Where there is no vision, the people are unrestrained, but happy is he who keeps the law.

9. Proverbs 21:5. The plans of the diligent lead surely to advantage.

10. Isaiah 33:6.   And He shall be the stability of your times, a wealth of salvation, wisdom, and knowledge; the fear of the Lord is his treasure.

11. Proverbs 23:7.   For as he thinks within himself, so he is.

12. Proverbs 24:16.   For a righteous man falls seven times and rises again.

13. Proverbs 11:25.   The generous man will be prosperous, and he who waters will himself be watered.

14. Second Peter 1:3–9.   Seeing that His divine power has granted to us everything pertaining to life and godliness, through the true knowledge of Him who called us by His own glory and excellence.

For by these He has granted to us His precious and magnificent promises, in order that by them you might become partakers of the divine nature, having escaped the corruption that is in the world by lust.

Now for this very reason also, applying all diligence, in your faith supply moral excellence, and in your moral excellence, knowledge;

and in your knowledge, self-control, and in your self-control, perseverance, and in your perseverance, godliness; and in your godliness, brotherly kindness, and in your brotherly kindness, Christian love.

For if these qualities are yours and are increasing, they render you neither useless nor unfruitful in the true knowledge of our Lord Jesus Christ.

For he who lacks these qualities is blind or short-sighted, having forgotten his purification from his former sins.

15. Philippians 4:13.   I can do all things through Him who strengthens me.

16. Proverbs 14:6.   Knowledge is easy to him who has understanding.

2

"I PROMISE"

Being in control of my life... Does that mean I can have anything I want?

That's right, as long as you are realistic in setting your goals. Do you know what you want out of life?

I want my family to be comfortable. I want my children to have a good education, which takes money. One thing I want is to prosper.[1]

That seems reasonable.

Sure, but how am I going to get it?

There are various ways. For one thing, you can use a gun and take what you want from other people.

I could never do that!

Well then, you can hire people and make them work hard, but refuse to pay them a decent wage. If they argue, you can fire them.

I wouldn't do that. Besides, I'm an employee. I work for someone else.

What about running up your debts? Have you tried using the magic words

"I PROMISE"?

What do you mean, "I promise"?

People like to buy new things because it makes them feel good. Often, these are things they can't afford. If they don't have enough money, they say the magic words, "I promise. Give me what I want. I promise that someday I'll pay you." This is called credit.[2]

Listen, I know all about credit.

I've been buying on credit for years. Now that I understand what you mean by "I promise," let me tell you:

Those are two of my favorite words in the English language.

I love the words . . .

I PROMISE.[3]

Most people do. It's nice to walk into a store and get what you want by repeating a magic formula. It's so nice that most people in this country have lost control of themselves. They've said it so many times that our country is drowning in promises.

We may soon reach a point where people will not accept our promises as they have in the past. Instead, they will press for repayment of outstanding loans. If that happens, many Americans could end up like the Richest Man in the World—going bankrupt and losing everything they have.[4]

I don't want that to happen to me or my family!

Of course you don't. But there is another way for you to get what you want out of life. This way is a little bit harder in the beginning because most people find it easier to take what they want than to do anything else. But if you want to be successful and see your desires fulfilled, you must learn

HOW TO GIVE.

The more you give in life, the more you will receive. Not many people know this, but those who do are among . . .

THE RICHEST PEOPLE IN THE WORLD.

America was built on the principle of giving. Over the centuries people came to this country, worked hard,[5] and produced huge amounts of wealth.[6] By following biblical principles, we became the richest nation in the world.

I remember hearing something about that in school. But why do we have so many problems if everybody in America is working hard to produce more wealth?

The problem is, they're not. Things have changed. People have forgotten how to work and how to give. Everyone wants to take instead. Everyone wants to get what they can while the getting is good. It doesn't occur to them that they should be producing goods and services equal to those they consume.

Many of us do not enjoy our work. We go into the office or factory without wanting to be there. It's just a job, right? A way to make money. Our heart isn't in our work, and we don't get very much done.[7]

Since it is no longer necessary to work in order to survive, many Americans do not bother to work at all.[8]

Look at our country. How many people do you think enjoy the work they do? How many are really productive?

Some people are productive—many farmers, for example. Farmers, who are a very small percentage of our population, raise enough food each year to feed the United States and half the world.

You're right. American farmers are very productive. I think I've taken them for granted. Whenever I go to the supermarket, I never think how someone went out and raised all that food. I just buy it.

We take many things for granted in this country. We take it for granted that we can pick up the telephone and call anywhere. We take television for granted since advances in electronics have made it available to everyone at a low cost.

People working with technology have developed computers that can do the work of thousands—storing information, transmitting knowledge, monitoring complex energy systems . . .

There are people within every field who are highly motivated and productive.

One person who comes to mind right now is my mechanic. Whenever I need work done on my car, I take it to him because I trust him. He's not just interested in money. He provides good service to all of his customers.

That is exactly what we are talking about. Different people are suited to different kinds of work. Some are born innovators. They enjoy thinking of new products that will benefit other members of society—things like solar technology, improved satellite communications, and better automotive designs. Others are good at organizing production. Other people are good at doing work that needs to be done, whether that means driving a bus, filming a television interview, or assembling CB radios. Whatever a person's line of work, it is useful if it produces a tangible benefit for other members of society. The better we do our job, the more we contribute to society, and the wealthier our nation will be.

What about teachers and artists?

Teachers are in a position to influence students and inspire them to make the most of their lives. They provide young people with basic skills, knowledge, and the ability to think creatively—all of which are necessary for success. By transmitting knowledge, teachers are important and productive members of society.

Artists inspire people to pay attention to the beauty in the world and to listen to the lessons life has to teach. Artists, musicians, dancers, poets, and other creative people inspire us to develop a more universal awareness, a kind of spiritual maturity.

This is very interesting. It seems that almost anyone can be productive.[9]

Yes, as long as they do a competent job and meet a real need in society.

In most jobs I know, there's not much room for creativity. The boss just tells you what to do, and you do it. If people were allowed to participate more, I think they could be more productive.

You're right. It is the responsibility of management, even more than labor, to improve productivity. We have something to learn from the Japanese in this. A lot of Japanese television sets, cars, cameras and computers are being sold in this country because their products are of high quality and relatively inexpensive.

Why is that?

Management and labor work together in Japan. They have learned to cooperate, and as a result, everyone is more efficient and productive.

The Japanese have tried something we have not thought of yet. They let their workers know that they are important, that they are part of a team, and that their cooperation is vital to the company they work for.

Japanese managers ask workers how they think a job should be done. They feel that people who do the work have useful information about how the job should be done. In this country, many employers think workers should follow orders, and that's it.

Why do they think that?

It is faster and easier to tell somebody what to do than it is to discuss it with them. It takes time to ask a worker how he or she thinks a job should be done. Once workers and managers sit down, though, and decide together how something should be done, the workers actually do a much better job. They feel more involved in their work because they share in the responsibility for it.

People feel more important when they influence the decisions that affect their lives. When people feel important, they try harder to do a good job.

That's true. But now, I have another question. You were talking about big machines and computers a while back, and saying how great they are. I don't understand how these new machines are good for me. They could put me out of work, couldn't they?

A few hundred years ago, buying a coat was as big an investment as buying a car today. Back then, coats had to be made by hand. Wool had to be hand-spun, cloth was woven by hand, and it took a great deal of time to make a coat. As soon as it became possible for people to produce coats quickly and easily with mechanical looms and sewing machines, the cost went way down. It became much easier for people to afford them, and all the people who had spent so much time weaving and sewing were now free to do other things.

But how did they find jobs? All they knew was how to make coats. A lot of my friends have lost jobs due to technology, and some of them are *still* out of work. I have one friend who works for a large corporation in this area. Two weeks ago, the management called a meeting of his whole division, and one hundred workers were told they would not have a job next month. My friend is so depressed that I don't know what to say to him.

Advances in technology can cause temporary discomfort for many people, particularly if they cannot see beyond what is happening at the moment. What is most important at times like this is to have the right attitude and to take a look at the larger picture.[10]

You may have to navigate some rapids to reach better times, but don't let this discourage you. While change is taking place, some people are conscious only of what they are losing. They do not see the prosperity they and everyone else will enjoy once the adjustment has been made.

Some people welcome change and benefit from it, while others resist all progress out of fear. IT MAKES SENSE, IF YOU WANT TO ENJOY LIFE IN THE YEARS AHEAD, TO BEGIN ADAPTING TO CHANGE NOW . . . because there will be plenty of change in the years to come.

Technology produces greater wealth for the entire country. It eliminates jobs in some sectors of the economy, but the total amount of wealth we produce increases. This greater wealth then leads to the creation of new jobs in other areas. With the old technology, many people have jobs which are boring and repetitive. Technology can free these people to find work which may ultimately be more fulfilling. Although it is usually jarring and uncomfortable to lose a job, people with a broader awareness can take advantage of the situation and find a new line of work which will bring them more happiness.

I still don't know what to tell my friend. He doesn't see the situation the way you do.

The best thing you can do is help him to believe in himself.[11]

If you are secure in your abilities, you know that losing a job is not the end of the world or the end of your working life. If you don't believe in yourself, however, any job loss will seem traumatic. When you believe in yourself, you know you can always find a job somewhere else, even if it is different from what you are doing now.

My younger brother is in a situation similar to your friend's, but he has a different attitude. He knows that the machine shop where he works may close in the coming months, but he believes in himself. He recently learned to use a sophisticated machine on which he programs computers to produce the machine parts his company needs. He enjoys his work and is paid well for what he does. He is always eager to learn something new, and his boss appreciates that.

Even if his shop closes in a few months, my brother knows he can find another job because he believes in himself. Either he'll find another job in the area, or he'll move. In fact, the last time I talked with him, he said he thought it would be exciting to see how it would be to live in another part of the country.

There are two ways you can look at any situation—either as an obstacle or as an opportunity for growth.

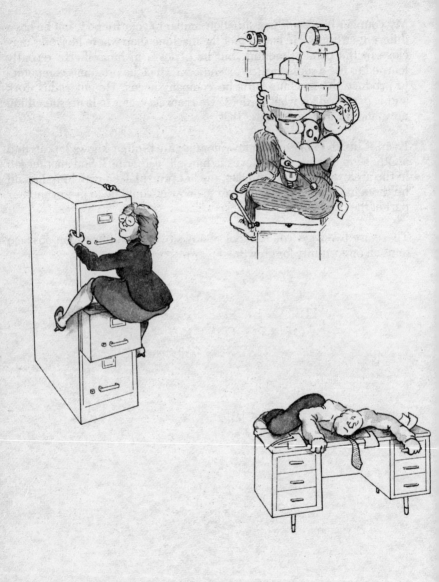

If you don't believe in yourself, the thought of losing your old job will totally shake you up.

IF YOU LOOK
AT THE LOSS OF A JOB
AS AN OPPORTUNITY FOR GROWTH,
IT CAN BE THE BEGINNING
OF A POSITIVE CHANGE
IN YOUR LIFE.

Your brother is in his twenties. My friend is 43 and much more set in his ways.

Every human being, regardless of age, has at his disposal the most powerful machine imaginable—a machine capable of performing feats that not even a computer can duplicate. That machine is called

THE HUMAN MIND.[12]

What about a person with several children to support? It won't be easy for them to make a change.

You're right. Changing jobs or careers when you have that kind of responsibility can be difficult. Still, people do it all the time. Generally, it would involve using your evenings and weekends for work, study or classes instead of recreation, but that would only be temporary. You just have to be motivated to change.

At work, most people use only one channel of their mind. After a while they begin to think it's the only channel there is. The truth of the matter, however, is that we each have many abilities. The more we experience different avenues of awareness and exercise each of our abilities, the more we can enjoy ourselves and our lives.

That's true. When I come home from work, I'm usually tired, but as soon as I get a hammer or a saw in my hand, suddenly I'm full of energy. I have never been able to understand that.

That's the way many people are. They have to drag themselves to work each morning because they don't really want to be there.[13]

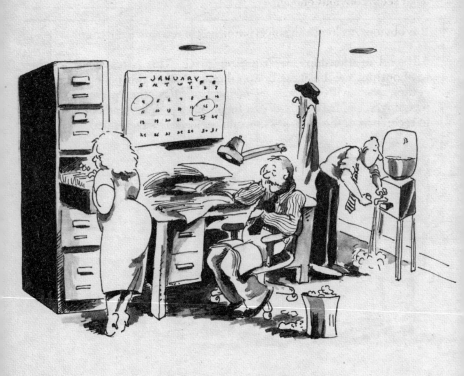

That's how it is at my job.

Compared with our *potential*, little real wealth is produced in America. However, we all want to consume whatever wealth there is.

We have come to feel entitled to prosperity and abundance. Somewhere along the road, we've lost sight of the fact that BEFORE ANYONE CAN CONSUME ANYTHING, SOMEONE MUST WORK TO PRODUCE IT.

That seems obvious enough.

It is obvious, as long as it suits your needs to recognize the truth.

All good relationships are based on giving. This is true whether the relationships are business or social ones. When two people come together, each with the idea of taking from the other person, nothing meaningful can happen between them. Both people stand back, waiting to receive from the other person, and each goes away disappointed.

If two people come to a picnic and each expects the other person to bring the food, nobody will have anything to eat.

However, when people come together with the idea of giving all they can to one another— whether on the job or in their personal lives—each person receives tremendously as a result.[14]

Think of the farmer. He has to plow, plant, and tend the crop before he can enjoy the fruit of his labor. He must devote time and energy to his work before the harvest.

Wouldn't it be unfair to approach that farmer, threaten him, and take most of what he has produced?[15]

Of course it would. That's ridiculous.

If you want to eat the farmer's food, you should pay him for it. It's the only fair thing to do.

We have a problem now in this country. We all want to enjoy the benefits of greater productivity, yet many of us refuse to do our share.[16]

Many of us live on credit instead of saving.

Special interest groups line up demanding favors from the government.[17]

And we elect politicians who promise to give us everything we want without worrying about how they will be able to pay for it.[18]

No one bothers to ask how Uncle Sam gets all the money he spends so freely.

Where does it come from?

IT COMES FROM THE PRODUCTIVE MEMBERS OF SOCIETY![19]

In order to transfer money to these special interest groups, government taxes the more productive members of society. The government takes money from your pocket and gives that money to people who have done little or nothing to earn it.

You make government sound unnecessary. Even evil.

We're not saying government is unnecessary or inherently evil. On the contrary, it is important to all of us. We just want to limit the size and function of government in order to prevent the abuses that have become commonplace in recent decades.

Then what should government do?

For one thing, *it should defend our country against foreign aggression.* The army exists to protect everyone's freedom. It is not meant to serve any special interest group.

Another function of government is to prevent people from harming one another. *It should maintain law and order.*

Can you be more specific about that?

The government should prevent people from robbing, cheating or killing one another. No one has the right to force anyone to do anything against their will.[20]

I won't argue with that.

For the same reason, we need legal safeguards to protect the environment. You can't have industry pouring chemicals into rivers and ruining our nation's water supply. That would threaten the life of every American.

I hope you're not one of those wacky environmentalists.

No, we're just wacky people who like to drink pure water and breathe clean air.

What else should government do?

It should build roads and maintain them.

Roads are used by everyone. Imagine if there were thousands of individual road owners in this country, each charging a toll to use their little stretch of highway.

That would be foolish.

Yes, just as it would be foolish for government to neglect other large projects which clearly provide huge benefits for society as a whole. At any point in time, there may be a few projects which are too large for any individual or private corporation to undertake but which benefit society as a whole. Government can undertake these projects, but *only* when the project is truly needed.

That makes sense, but who would take care of those who are in need?

If anyone in society was truly helpless and could not take care of him or herself, we would not want them to suffer.[21] First it is the family's responsibility.[22] If the family can't provide for them, then the responsibility would be with the church.

What about people who just say they're helpless?

That's a good question. Few people are truly helpless. After all, if handicapped people can learn to function and lead productive lives, why can't people who are much less disadvantaged? The problem must be in their minds.

Too many people don't believe in themselves. They don't believe in their ability to adapt to change. If a man is a machinist, he sees himself as being only that. He can't IMAGINE himself doing anything else. Even if he can see himself doing something more creative and enjoyable, he is often afraid to try.

But what if there is no longer a need for his services? He has to be retrained for another job, doesn't he?

Not if he says he's helpless.

How can he be helpless?

He won't actually *be* helpless. But if he loses his job due to automation or foreign competition, he can scream to the government and say he needs help. If the government buys his story, then even *he'll* believe that it's true.

Many large corporations are doing the same thing. They lose money year after year, so they ask government for import quotas, subsidies, and federally guaranteed loans. They need help to stay in business. When government steps in to help these companies, however, it perpetuates the situation it wants to eradicate: lack of self-sufficiency. It taxes successful businesses in order to support unsuccessful ones and thus ruins the economy.

After all, if a bankrupt company is bailed out by the government, what incentive is there for its workers to find jobs in more productive, profitable sectors of the economy? Why should they move on when they are being encouraged to stay where they are, poor productivity or not?

That doesn't make sense at all. It seems crazy.

Unfortunately, it happens all the time. Individuals and businesses are constantly saying to the government, "I'm helpless. Subsidize me."[23]

They are afraid to change, even if it will lead to something better.

The nature of life is to grow, and growth takes place through change. You see this all the time in plants, trees, and creative human beings. People who are holding on to jobs that are no longer useful are afraid to embrace change and all the new opportunities it can offer.

Sometimes you get on the philosophical side, but I have to admit, you've made some good points. Sometimes I hold on to views that are no longer useful. They're comfortable, like an old shoe. Maybe the shoe is stretched out and doesn't fit anymore, but still it's familiar.

What happens to a country when too many people believe they are helpless?

Those who are helpless demand that the government take care of them. Then, people who work and pay taxes are forced to support those who refuse to work.[24] As time passes fewer people produce, while more and more people make demands on the government.

The size of the national pie begins shrinking, and soon everybody is
fighting to get a piece, just a small piece, of what has been produced.

They don't realize that if they were to turn around and produce, there would be more than enough for everyone.

Instead of cooperating and *working*[25] to solve our problems, everyone wants to blame someone else for what they see is wrong with our economy. Everyone is pointing a finger.

WHO DO YOU LIKE TO BLAME?

Some people say our standard of living is falling because of the Arabs, or the oil companies, the Russians, big business, labor, welfare, or the government.

Well, who is to blame?

WE ARE. ALL OF US TOGETHER. OUR BEHAVIOR HAS CAUSED THE FALL IN PRODUCTIVITY IN AMERICA, AND THE RESULT IS A DECLINE IN OUR STANDARD OF LIVING.

Wait a minute! I'm not sure I understand all this talk about inflation, unemployment, bankruptcy and debt. But what you have just said gives me the feeling that this country can be turned around.[26]

After all, if we're the problem, all we need to do is understand what we have done wrong and correct the mistakes we have made. What we have to do is change ourselves.

IF WE CAN SUCCEED AT THAT, WE CAN ONCE AGAIN
BECOME THE MOST PROSPEROUS PEOPLE IN THE WORLD.[27]

NOTES

1. Proverbs 3:13,16.   How blessed is the man who finds wisdom, and the man who gains understanding.

   Long life is in her right hand; in her left hand are riches and honor.

   Proverbs 22:4.   The reward for humility and the fear of the Lord are riches, honor and life.

2. Romans 13:8.   Owe nothing to anyone except to love one another.

3. Proverbs 22:26.   Do not be among those who give pledges, among those who become sureties for debts. If you have nothing with which to pay, why should he take your bed from under you?

4. Nehemiah 5:1–5.   Now there was a great outcry of the people and of their wives against their Jewish brothers.

   For there were those who said, "We, our sons and our daughters, are many; therefore let us get grain that we may eat and live."

   Also there were others who said, "We are mortgaging our fields, our vineyards, and our houses that we might get grain because of the famine."

   Also there were those who said, "We have borrowed money for the king's tax on our fields and our vineyards.

   "And now our flesh is like the flesh of our brothers, our children like their children. Yet behold, we are forcing our sons and our daughters to be slaves, and some of our daughters are forced into bondage already, and we are helpless because our fields and vineyards belong to others."

5. Proverbs 14:23.   In all labor there is profit, but mere talk leads only to poverty.

6. Ecclesiastes 5:19.   Furthermore, as for every man to whom God has given riches and wealth, He has also empowered him to eat from them and to receive his reward and rejoice in his labor; this is the gift of God.

7. Ecclesiastes 9:10. Whatever your hand finds to do, verily, do it with all your might.

8. Second Thessalonians 3:11. For we hear that some among you are leading an undisciplined life, doing no work at all.

   Second Corinthians 9:6. Now this I say, he who sows sparingly shall also reap sparingly, and he who sows bountifully shall also reap bountifully.

9. Proverbs 12:27. The precious possession of a man is diligence.

10. Proverbs 23:18. Surely there is a future, and your hope will not be cut off.

11. Proverbs 27:17. Iron sharpens iron, so one man sharpens another.

   Proverbs 23:7. For as he thinks within himself, so he is.

12. Romans 12:2. And do not be conformed to this world, but be transformed by the renewing of your mind.

13. Proverbs 18:9. He who is slack in his work is brother to him who destroys.

14. Luke 6:38. Give, and it will be given to you; good measure, pressed down, shaken together, running over they will pour into your lap. For whatever measure you deal out to others, it will be dealt to you in return.

15. Second Timothy 2:6. The hard working farmer ought to be the first to receive his share of the crops.

   Exodus 20:15. You shall not steal.

16. Second Thessalonians 3:10. For even when we were with you, we used to give you this order: if anyone will not work, neither let him eat.

17. Galatians 2:6. God shows no partiality.

18. Proverbs 22:3. The prudent sees the evil and hides himself, but the naive go on, and are punished for it.

Proverbs 29:20.   Do you see the man who is hasty in his words? There is more hope for a fool than for him.

19. Second Thessalonians 3:8.   Nor did we eat anyone's bread without paying for it, but with labor and hardship we kept working night and day so that we might not be a burden to any of you.

20. Romans 13:1.   For there is no authority except from God.

21. Romans 15:26.   For Macedonia and Achaia have been pleased to make a contribution for the poor among the saints in Jerusalem.

22. First Timothy 5:8.   But if anyone does not provide for his own, and especially for those of his household, he has denied the faith, and is worse than an unbeliever.

23. Second Thessalonians 3:12.   Now such persons we command and exhort in the Lord Jesus Christ to work in quiet fashion and eat their own bread.

24. Second Thessalonians 3:7–9.   For you yourselves know how you ought to follow our example, because we did not act in an undisciplined manner among you,

nor did we eat anyone's bread without paying for it, but with labor and hardship we kept working night and day so that we might not be a burden to any of you;

not because we do not have the right to this, but in order to offer ourselves as a model for you, that you might follow our example.

25. Proverbs 10:4.   Poor is he who works with a negligent hand, but the hand of the diligent makes rich.

26. Second Chronicles 7:14.   And if My people who are called by My name humble themselves and pray, and seek My face and turn from their wicked ways, then I will hear from heaven, will forgive their sins, and will heal their land.

27. Deuteronomy 28:1.   Now it shall be, if you will diligently obey the Lord your God, being careful to do all His commandments which I command you today, the Lord your God will set you high above all the nations of the earth.

3

THE TRUTH
ABOUT INFLATION

You say that we are all responsible for the problems of inflation and unemployment, yet I don't see what I have to do with any of this. Can you tell me what I am doing wrong?

Like most Americans, you probably consume more than you produce. You want to lead a comfortable life, yet you may not have enough money left, after taxes, to buy all the things you want. So you spend everything you earn and may even go into debt to buy what you want. Isn't that true?

I never seem to have much money at the end of the month, and sometimes I have to use my credit cards to get by. But is there anything wrong with that? I thought the government wants us to spend money. Isn't that good for the economy?[1]

If carried to an extreme, spending can have serious consequences. Imagine what would happen to a farmer whose family ate more food than he was able to produce. If the farmer didn't save some seeds from his harvest each fall, he wouldn't have anything to plant the next spring.

That's obvious, but what does that have to do with me?

The size of our "national pie" depends on how much wealth we produce each year. If you think of America as a large farm, producing not only food but also automobiles, steel, computers, television sets, and housing; it will be easy to understand this concept. Each year a lot of wealth is created, far more than is produced in India, China, or the Soviet Union. But we also consume much more than people do in those countries. You eat your slice of the pie. Your neighbor eats his. Government takes its share, and

NOT MUCH IS LEFT TO REINVEST IN OUR ECONOMY!

What difference does that make?

Productivity erodes as a result. When no one invests in new factories and machines, economic growth slows to a halt. We all feel the effects of that—there is less wealth to go around. You see, savings are crucial to our economy. It takes money to build a new factory, or to upgrade an old one. It takes time, energy, and money to produce anything in this world.

122

For generations, Americans saved a portion of their income and reinvested it in the economy to produce new goods, rather than spending their entire income on consumer items. The result of this was to produce a vast amount of wealth in America. As a consequence of these investments, a huge amount of technology was developed.

By not saving and by living beyond our means, we have created a terrible problem in the economy. If you're not saving part of your income and channeling it into productive investment, you are depriving the economy of what it needs to produce greater wealth in the future. Without investments to improve productivity, our economy will gradually deteriorate. That will reduce the standard of living for everyone.

It's not so difficult to save and invest, either. It's just a habit people get into, or sometimes fall out of.[2] In many parts of the world, people are in the habit of saving a large part of their income. In those countries, like Germany and Japan, where money is saved and invested in new factories, research, and technology, the level of productivity and the people's standard of living continue to rise.

But it's hard to save money when taxes and inflation are so high!

We are caught in an awful bind. In addition to changing ourselves, we need to change the laws which discourage people from saving.

What about those All-Savers Certificates we heard about a few years ago? Were they a step in the right direction?

All-Savers Certificates were a stopgap measure to prevent weak savings and loans and banks from going out of business. The real solution to our problem is to reduce taxes—by cutting government spending—and to eliminate inflation altogether.

At that point, when people are free to save and invest their money as they see fit—without worrying about inflation or the IRS—they will put their money to work quite naturally. We won't need artificial incentives to encourage people to save and invest in new factories, research, or technology. That will all happen spontaneously. Investment, productivity, and our standard of living will all rise as soon as we eliminate the obstacles to saving.

What is productivity, anyway?

Productivity is output. It measures your ability to create something of use to society. The more goods or better service you provide your employer, the greater your productivity is and the greater his profits will be.[3]

What do I care how much profit I make for my employer?

Your employer can only increase your pay out of his profits. The more profits you make for your employer, the more he has to share with you.

But my boss hasn't given me a raise for the past three years, except to keep up with inflation. Whenever the company's profits rise, they don't share any of it with me.

Just as there are good workers and bad workers, there are good employers and bad employers. What the selfish employers have in common with irresponsible workers is that they use other people. They take something without giving what it is worth in return.[4]

The bad worker tries to do as little as he can and get paid as much as possible.[5]

The bad employer, no matter how much profit he makes, tries to pay his workers as little as possible.[6]

In both cases, everybody loses. The poor worker never gets ahead in life and never accomplishes what he is capable of achieving. He cheats himself of the opportunity to do his best and to grow.[7] Likewise, the bad employer never learns how to get what he wants by winning the cooperation of other people. He must fight with his workers over pay and try to force them to produce as much as possible.

When you treat people poorly, they don't work as well as they can. You are actually *lowering* your profits. The Japanese know this. It is one of the keys to their phenomenal success in today's economy. The Japanese emphasize harmony, mutual benefit, cooperation, and trust as the keys to prosperity for their entire work force—for labor as well as for management.

Some Japanese firms have even bought American factories—factories plagued by low worker morale, absenteeism, and product deficiency— and have turned these factories around, using the same work force to produce better products, in greater quantity, at a much lower cost.

How did they do it?

They treat each employee with respect. They make people feel that the work they do is important, and as a result, people begin to take pride in their work. Even more important, the Japanese take responsibility for each person they hire. When you accept a job with a particular company, it's like joining a family. You share in the company's profits during good years, and have job security when times are rough. Workers retrain for a different job if necessary, but they are not fired when business is slow.

Under conditions like these, workers naturally cooperate with a company's management. They have a vested interest in doing their best since they share in the company's profits, but they also have a responsibility to meet since management is treating them well.

That's a far cry from the way things are in America.

Most people I know don't like the work they're doing. They don't feel a sense of responsibility towards their job or do the best they can because it doesn't interest them. They're just putting in time to earn a living. As a result, they are not very productive. They don't make much money or enjoy life nearly as much as they could. No wonder we're faced with falling productivity.[8]

You are pointing out a real need for change. Fortunately, many American companies have already learned how to win the cooperation of their employees by treating them with dignity and respect. Many of the high technology companies on the West Coast provide their employees with good benefits, job security, and wages that are consistent with production and profits. Yet for the most part, we still have a long way to go in America.

Let's get back to the idea of savings, though.

If I earned more or if the government didn't take so much of my salary in taxes, I could save. But I don't see how my savings would make any impression on the larger picture.

If you were the only one saving, it would not. Likewise, if you were the only one living on credit, that wouldn't matter either. One person spending more than he or she earns will not hurt anyone, at least not enough to notice. But there are many people in America today who do not produce enough goods to pay for those they wish to consume. To fill the gap, they turn to credit and government spending.

This has been going on for years. BY NOW, AMERICA HAS REACHED THE POINT WHERE WE CONSUME MORE WEALTH THAN WE PRODUCE—YEAR AFTER YEAR.

How is that possible?

We have been living off savings from the past, and we have been buying more goods from abroad than we produce and export.

How do we cover the difference between what we buy and sell?

We give our creditors paper dollars, which soon lose their value through inflation.[9]

That must make them unhappy!

You're right. But at the moment, there isn't much they can do since the dollar is the world's key currency.

What do you mean by "the world's key currency"?

It means the dollar is treated the same way gold used to be, as a standard of international exchange. It is the only currency large enough —and presumably stable enough—to be used in this way.

From what you've been saying, it doesn't sound like that works anymore.

It doesn't. Since the American government can print as many dollars as it wants—reducing the value of every other dollar in circulation— American currency is not a reliable store of value.[10] This is true for people in this country, as well as for someone in Argentina, Burma or Brazil. It *is* better than other currencies, though. Every other currency in the world is either less reliable than the dollar, or too limited in quantity to serve as a medium of international exchange. As a result, we are able to go on printing money to pay for our imports and to live way beyond our means.

What will happen if we keep this up?

At some point, people will decide they do not want to own dollars anymore. We will have runaway inflation, and our currency will become worthless. Already, we see signs of deterioration in our economy in the form of continual recessions and unemployment. Productivity is falling, unemployment is high, and we find ourselves plagued by inflation.

What causes inflation anyway?

If you look in the dictionary, you will find inflation defined as "an increase in the volume of money and credit relative to available goods resulting in a substantial and continuing rise in the general price level."[11] In other words, inflation is defined as an increase in the supply of money.

Although most people equate rising prices with inflation, *the actual cause of higher prices is inflation of the money supply*. Price inflation is the *result* of money inflation.

By relying on credit and government spending to fulfill our many desires, we have painted ourselves into a corner from which it will be difficult to escape. Taxes are already so high that it's hard for people to save their money and to invest. And, as we have said, the expansion of consumer credit also causes prices to rise.

How does that happen?

When people save their money and use these savings to increase productivity, more goods become available for people to buy. As a result, prices go down. But if instead, productivity is falling and people borrow money to buy whatever goods are available, prices are bound to go up. You have more money chasing fewer goods. Higher prices are inevitable.

This situation is aggravated by our banking and credit system, known as the *fractional reserve*. For each dollar that your bank has on deposit with the Federal Reserve, IT CAN CREATE AND LEND EIGHT DOLLARS TO ITS CUSTOMERS.

$8.00? Where does all this money come from? You'd better explain this to me.

Banks are in the business of lending money. They want to lend customers as much money as possible in order to maximize the amount of interest they receive.[12] The government cooperates by saying that a bank can lend as much money as it wants, as long as it keeps a fraction[13] of its loan on deposit with the Federal Reserve.[14]

Under the fractional reserve system, your bank is allowed to create money out of thin air!

You mean it actually prints money and lends it out?

No. It doesn't need to. The bank simply makes a computer entry. Under this system, creating money is nothing but a series of computer entries. Your bank is lending money that does not really exist.

What if the borrower wants cash?

Then your bank makes another computer entry at the office of the Federal Reserve. It receives Federal Reserve Notes, which it gives to the customer who demanded cash.

Where do these Federal Reserve Notes come from?

They are printed by the Federal Reserve, *which is allowed by law to create as much paper money as it wants.* As a result, your bank makes a profit collecting interest on all these loans, while consumers are left to face the consequences: rising prices and debt.

This is outrageous! Why does the government let it happen?

Special interests have a great deal of influence in our government. Groups which profit from inflation—for example, banks, real estate brokers, and many large corporations—spend a fortune each year lobbying in Washington, trying to expand their special privileges. Since we do not speak out and oppose them, their interests prevail, and *we* get stuck with the bill.[15]

I don't see why we let them get away with it. There must be something we get out of the deal.

There is: an *illusion* of prosperity.

When banks lend out more money than they have on deposit, an artificial boom is created. Suddenly, everyone feels rich. We have money in our pockets, and if we want something, we can go out and buy it.

The only problem is that there is no more wealth in society than there was before. More money is circulating, but the amount of goods for sale has not increased proportionately. Prices rise, since under the circumstances, the value of money must go down.

We don't gain anything in the long run, but the special interests do, and so do the politicians who support them.

What do the politicians get?

They get re-elected each time they run for office since the special interests they represent finance their re-election campaign. Or if they lose, they are often given a government job or work in an established corporation or law firm. Why would anyone help a few people at the expense of many, unless they were to benefit in the process?

I don't want that kind of person in office!

Then you should check the voting records of your Senators and Congressional Representatives. They should not be in office if they have made a career out of supporting special interest legislation.

It is vital that we reject the politics of special interest, *even if the special interests we reject are our own.* We must elect men and women who have no political debts and who will not be persuaded—by whatever group talks the loudest or spends the most money—to pass a law that taxes all of us in order to benefit a select few.[16]

Before 1913, there was a limit to how much banks could inflate our nation's money supply. The dollar was backed by gold. In fact, it *was* gold: the word "dollar" meant 25.8 grains of gold, 9/10 pure. Whenever you deposited your money in a bank, you were depositing a fixed quantity of gold.

Of course, the bank could still lend money. It could issue receipts for the gold held in its vaults. It could even issue more receipts than the amount of gold it had on deposit. This was frequently done.

People who borrowed money would use these receipts to make purchases, and others would accept them, reasoning, "If these are receipts for gold, they must be *as good as gold* itself." No one in the community had any way of knowing a receipt was not fully backed by gold until prices started to rise, and it became difficult to pass a receipt on to someone else at face value.

At that point, people would suddenly panic. Everyone would run to the bank and demand gold in exchange for their receipts, only to find that the bank did not have enough gold to meet all of their demands.

Banks would collapse. People who had a lot of receipts would lose their money, and a depression would follow as business came to a temporary standstill.

This entire cycle—the "business cycle" of boom and bust—was caused by a reckless expansion of credit. The depressions which followed an inflation of the money supply were sharp and painful.

Yet, our current situation is even worse. The fractional reserve system is still in operation today. The inflation of paper money is still going on—only now we don't have any easy way to stop it. The automatic controls are all gone.

What controls are gone? What do you mean?

As long as we were operating under a gold standard, neither the government nor private banks could inflate the money supply for long.

What is the gold standard?

Under a gold standard, all paper money that is issued must be backed by a fixed quantity of gold. When the United States was on the gold standard, all paper money could be exchanged for gold upon demand.

At that time, the only real money was gold. Paper could serve as a convenient substitute, yet paper was never more than a *receipt* for real money. At any time, paper dollars could be exchanged for gold.

Whenever prices started to rise and people became anxious, they demanded gold. If a bank issued more receipts than it had gold, then its receipts might become worthless. But the dollar—25.8 grains of gold—maintained its purchasing power through the years.[17]

Today, however, you can no longer exchange a twenty dollar bill for a twenty dollar gold coin. All of our money is made of paper. The dollar has been *divorced* from gold, and little pieces of paper, manufactured overnight by a bank or by the government, have as much purchasing power as the money you have worked hard all year to earn.

How did that happen?

Everyone knew how much hardship was caused by the business cycle—the cycle of inflationary boom and bust. Back in 1913, the government decided to moderate this cycle and bring it under control.

That sounds like a good idea, but how did they do it?

First, Congress created the Federal Reserve. Then, in 1933, we abandoned the gold standard. Rather than prevent artificial booms from occurring, WE DECIDED TO AVOID THE BUST!

Instead of telling bankers, "Don't lend more money than you have on deposit, or you will start an artificial boom," government eliminated the convertibility of paper money into gold—thereby granting banks and government almost unlimited power to inflate our money supply.

We let that happen? Why?

We were told this would end the cycle of boom and bust, and lead to permanent prosperity. Not knowing any better, we agreed to give it a try.[18] You see . . .

People get "high" from credit expansion. The early stages of inflation are like a big party. The only problem is, sooner or later you start to come down.

When that happens—when the supply of new money runs short and a recession sets in—people line up and demand a fresh dose of credit to keep the party going.

We eliminated the convertibility of paper into gold and created the
Federal Reserve to keep this inflationary house of cards from falling.
Now, fresh supplies of money can be pumped into the economy to avoid
depressions, so long as we are willing to pay the price—continued
inflation and a rising mountain of debt.

Can this go on indefinitely?

Everyone knows you can borrow for a while without anything serious happening.

But at some point, after debts have piled up...

the floor will collapse under the weight of all those obligations.

What do you mean, collapse?

We are referring to either a loss of confidence in paper money, causing runaway inflation, or to a depression, where people are unable to repay their debts. We're talking about the breakdown of our economy.

By increasing the supply of money and expanding credit even more, you can avoid the pain of a depression for a while. But at some point, inflation will get out of control, and there will be a cry from the people of this country to stop it.

How do you do that?

You stop inflation by not increasing the money supply. But then, the recession you were trying to avoid suddenly appears. People find they cannot afford to buy so many goods, jobs are lost, and some people can't repay their debts.

This is getting scary. I feel trapped. What can I do? What *should* we do?

We have to get back on the path of financial responsibility as soon as possible. Once you step off this path, you have nothing but problems.

This is especially true for a nation as a whole. When you abandon the path of fiscal responsibility, it's like trading a well-built house for one that always needs repair.

If we do not act soon, the consequences could be disastrous. We have moved beyond the early, pleasant stage of our addiction to easy money and are now faced with the threat of runaway inflation or the pain of another major depression.

We have only one sane choice before us. We must kick the habit of inflation as quickly, and gently, as possible.

Most of this is obvious, but what about the Federal Reserve?

The Federal Reserve puts a tremendous amount of power in the hands of a few individuals. *The people who control the Federal Reserve control our entire economy.* Their decisions to increase or decrease the supply of money in America determine whether there will be an inflationary boom or a sudden catastrophic depression.

Yet, despite all this power, they are not responsible to anyone. They are not responsible to the President; they are not responsible to Congress; and they are not responsible to the American people.[19] In fact, although the Federal Reserve has been in existence for nearly 70 years—presiding over two depressions, eight recessions, and the most prolonged inflation in American history—its actions have never once been audited and brought to public view.

To give so much power to a handful of men who are not accountable for their actions is inconsistent with our form of government. If there were no Federal Reserve, there could be no sustained inflation. The only way you can have prolonged inflation is to have a central bank with a monopoly on a nation's money supply.

For the next few years, we must perform a delicate balancing act. We must avoid both hyperinflation and deflation as we seek to move beyond the danger now confronting us.

Once we take the necessary steps, however, the bad times will be over. We can then rebuild our economy on solid ground.

NOTES

1. Romans 13:8.   Owe nothing to anyone except to love one another.

2. First Corinthians 16:2.   On the first day of every week let each one of you put aside and save, as he may prosper.

3. Proverbs 14:23.   In all labor there is profit, but mere talk leads only to poverty.

4. James 5:1–4.   Come now, you rich, weep and howl for your miseries which are coming upon you.

   Your riches have rotted and your garments have become moth-eaten.

   Your gold and your silver have rusted; and their rust will be a witness against you and will consume your flesh like fire. It is in the last days that you have stored up your treasure!

   Behold, the pay of the laborers who mowed your fields, and which has been withheld by you, cries out against you; and the outcry of those who did the harvesting has reached the ears of the Lord of Sabaoth.

5. Proverbs 18:9.   He also who is slack in his work is brother to him who destroys.

6. James 5:4.   Behold, the pay of the laborers who mowed your fields, and which has been withheld by you, cries out against you; and the outcry of those who did the harvesting has reached the ears of the Lord of Sabaoth.

7. Proverbs 10:4.   Poor is he who works with a negligent hand, but the hand of the diligent makes rich.

8. Ecclesiastes 9:10.   Whatever your hand finds to do, verily, do it with all your might.

9. Proverbs 20:23.   Differing weights are an abomination to the Lord, but a just weight is His delight.

10. Proverbs 11:1. A false balance is an abomination to the Lord, but a just weight is His delight.

11. *Webster's Third New International Dictionary of the English Language* (Springfield, Massachusetts: G & C Merriam Company, 1981), p. 1159.

Commentary on the Definition of Inflation by Ralph Smeed:

The authors of this book are very much concerned about the interpretation of words—and rightly so. In Twentieth Century America, the establishment's interpretation of one word, *inflation*, is tearing at the very foundation of our system of economic enterprise. It can be seen by the simple juxtaposition of two interpretations of the same word. A rare thing happens with this word. No matter which definition is used, it has an exactly opposite, not merely different, meaning in terms of coming to grips with a solution to the problem of inflation.

One definition points logically and squarely at the individual (i.e., the entrepreneur) as the bad guy causing high prices. The other definition points logically and squarely at the collective (i.e., the government) as the bad guy causing high prices. The use of these two definitions has brought about a classic example of what the great Ludwig von Mises calls the "semantic jungle."

Today's high prices are the inevitable result of more and more artificial money chasing up the price of goods and services. More money being printed by government increases the money supply. That's inflation. That's bad. More money saved by individuals out of their production is how capital is formed. That money does not inflate. That's good. Whichever definition we accept, however, we should remember that we cannot have our cake and eat it too.

Government prints money. Individuals produce goods. Notice how slick the following definitions of inflation work to point out (or avoid) who is at fault. The definitions either point to the government's responsibility or to the individual's responsibility. Interestingly enough, the two definitions tend to be mutually exclusive in terms of identifying our culprit.

One definition defines inflation as the increase in prices. Therefore, using this definition, any intelligent person would logically reason, since prices are so high and since the entrepreneur places the price tag on his goods or services, that the high prices must be his fault.

Consequently, we reason that wage and price controls of some kind must be applied by government to curb runaway prices.

The other definition states that inflation is the increase in the quantity of money or money substitutes (usually followed by a rise in the general price level). Since our Constitution gives Congress the absolute power to coin money and regulate the value thereof, it has been interpreted to be legal, if not moral, for the government to do this and to print almost unlimited quantities of money and to increase credit whenever politically expedient. This the government is presently doing in a way that not one person in one thousand can detect.

An overabundance of money is like an oversupply of anything else: its value decreases. Therefore, the money we have in our paycheck or savings account buys less. Since the government "counterfeiters" are printing feverishly almost day and night, prices will not come down unless and until we decide which interpretation of the word *inflation* we want our lawmakers to use.

Until our politicians view the proliferation of the supply of money and credit as the *real* evil behind our problem of inflation—by whatever definition—the present policy of too much government will not even be slowed down. Prices of everything will go through the roof.

Thus, we will continue to outlaw or render impotent the pricing system as a method for signaling those of us who produce and save when to produce more and when to produce less, when to save more and when to save less. It is only when producers save that capital is formed, making it available to help employees to produce more so that they too can save for a rainy day. That rainy day may now be upon us, as a bad storm, due in large part to past interpretations and definitions of one word—*inflation*.

Ralph Smeed, President, Center for the Study of Market Alternatives, P.O. Box 1001, Caldwell, Idaho 83605.

12. Deuteronomy 23:19.   You shall not charge interest to your countrymen: interest on money, food, or anything that may be loaned at interest.

13. 12.5%

14. "Inflating by simply printing more money is now considered old-fashioned. For one thing, it is too *visible*; with a lot of high-

denomination bills floating around, the public might get the trouble some idea that the cause of the unwelcome inflation is the government's printing of all the bills—and the government might be stripped of that power. Instead, governments have come up with a much more complex and sophisticated, and much less visible, means of doing the same thing: of organizing increases in the money supply to give themselves more money to spend and to subsidize favored political groups. The idea was this: instead of stressing the printing of money, retain the paper dollars or marks or francs as the basic money (the "legal tender"), and then pyramid on top of that a mysterious and invisible, but no less potent, "checkbook money," or bank demand deposits. The result is an inflationary engine, controlled by government, which no one but bankers, economists, and government central bankers understands—and designedly so.

First, it must be realized that the entire commercial banking system, in the United States or elsewhere, is under the total control of the central government—a control that the banks welcome, for it permits them to create money. The banks are under the complete control of the central bank—a government institution—a control stemming largely from the central bank's compulsory monopoly over the printing of money. In the United States, the Federal Reserve System performs this central banking function. The Federal Reserve ("the Fed") then permits the commercial banks to pyramid bank demand deposits ("checkbook money") on top of their own "reserves" (deposits at the Fed) by a multiple of approximately 8:1. In other words, if bank reserves at the Fed increase by $1 billion, the banks can and do pyramid their deposits by $8 billion—that is, the banks create $8 billion worth of new money.

Why do bank demand deposits constitute the major part of the money supply? Officially, they are not money or legal tender in the way that Federal Reserve Notes are money. But they constitute a promise by a bank that it will redeem its demand deposits in cash (Federal Reserve Notes) anytime that the deposit holder (the owner of the "checking account") may desire. The point, of course, is that the banks *don't have* the money; they cannot, since they owe eight times their reserves, which are their own checking account at the Fed. The public, however, is induced to trust the banks by the penumbra of soundness and sanctity laid about them by the Federa'

Reserve System. For the Fed can and does bail out banks in trouble. If the public understood the process and descended in a storm upon the banks demanding their money, the Fed, in a pinch, if it wanted, could always *print* enough money to tide the banks over.

The Fed, then, controls the rate of monetary inflation by adjusting the multiple (8:1) of bank money creations, or, more importantly, by determining the total amount of bank reserves. In other words, if the Fed wishes to increase the total money supply by $8 billion, instead of actually printing the $8 billion, it will contrive to increase bank reserves by $1 billion, and then leave it up to the banks to create $8 billion of new checkbook money. The public, meanwhile, is kept ignorant of the process or of its significance.

How do the banks create new deposits? Simply by lending them out in the process of creation. Suppose, for example, that the banks receive the $1 billion of new reserves; the banks will lend out $8 billion and create the new deposits in the course of making these new loans. In short, when the commercial banks lend money to an individual, a business firm, or the government, they are *not* relending existing money that the public laboriously had saved and deposited in their vaults—as the public usually believes. They lend out new demand deposits that they create in the course of the loan—and they are limited only by the "reserve requirements," by the required maximum multiple of deposit to reserves (e.g., 8:1). For, after all, they are not printing paper dollars or digging up pieces of gold; they are simply issuing deposit or "checkbook" claims upon themselves for cash—claims which they wouldn't have a prayer of honoring if the public as a whole should ever rise up at once and demand such a settling of their accounts.

How, then, does the Fed contrive to determine (almost always, to *increase*) the total reserves of the commercial banks? It can and does *lend* reserves to the banks, and it does so at an artificially cheap rate (the "rediscount rate"). But still, the banks do not like to be heavily in debt to the Fed, and so the total loans outstanding from the Fed to the banks is never very high. By far the most important route for the Fed's determining of total reserves is little known or understood by the public: the method of "open market purchases." What this simply means is that the Federal Reserve Bank goes out into the open market and buys an asset. Strictly, it doesn't matter what kind

of an asset the Fed buys. It could, for example, be a pocket calc
lator for twenty dollars. Suppose that the Fed buys a pocket calcu
lator from XYZ Electronics for twenty dollars. The Fed acquires
calculator; but the important point for our purposes is that XYZ
Electronics acquires a check for twenty dollars from the Federa
Reserve Bank. Now, the Fed is not open to checking accounts from
private citizens, only from banks and the federal government itself
XYZ Electronics, therefore, can only do one thing with its twenty
dollar check: deposit it at its own bank, say the Acme Bank. At thi
point, another transaction takes place: XYZ gets an increase c
twenty dollars in its checking account, in its "demand deposits." I
return, Acme Bank gets a check, made over to itself, from th
Federal Reserve Bank.

Now, the first thing that has happened is that XYZ's money stock ha
gone up by twenty dollars—its newly increased account at the Acm
Bank—and nobody else's money stock has changed at all. So, at th
end of this initial phase—phase I—the money supply has increase
by twenty dollars, the same amount as the Fed's purchase of a
asset. If one asks, where did the Fed get the twenty dollars to bu
the calculator, then the answer is: it created the twenty dollars ou
of thin air by simply writing out a check upon itself. No one, neithe
the Fed nor anyone else, *had* the twenty dollars before it was cre
ated in the process of the Fed's expenditure.

But this is not all. For now the Acme Bank, to its delight, finds it ha
a check on the Federal Reserve. It rushes to the Fed, deposits it
and acquires an increase of $20 in its reserves, that is, in its "deman
deposits with the Fed." Now that the banking system has an ir
crease in $20, it can and does expand credit, that is create mor
demand deposits in the form of loans to business (or to consumers c
government), until the total increase in checkbook money is $16(
At the end of phase II, then, we have an increase of $20 in ban
reserves generated by Fed purchase of a calculator for that amoun
an increase in $160 in bank demand deposits, and an increase of $14
in bank loans to business or others. The total money supply h;
increased by $160, of which $140 was created by the banks in th
course of lending out checkbook money to business, and $20 w;
created by the Fed in the course of buying the calculator.

In practice, of course, the Fed does not spend much of its tim
buying haphazard assets. Its purchases of assets are so huge in orde

to inflate the economy that it must settle on a regular, highly liquid asset. In practice, this means purchases of U.S. government bonds and other U.S. government securities. The U.S. government bond market is huge and highly liquid, and the Fed does not have to get into the political conflicts that would be involved in figuring out which private stocks or bonds to purchase. For the government, this process also has the happy consequence of helping to prop up the government security market, and keep up the price of government bonds.

Suppose, however, that some bank, perhaps under the pressure of its depositors, might have to cash in some of its checking account reserves in order to acquire hard currency. What would happen to the Fed then, since its checks had created new bank reserves out of thin air? Wouldn't it be forced to go bankrupt or the equivalent? No, because the Fed has a monopoly on the printing of cash, and it could—and would—simply redeem its demand deposit by printing whatever Federal Reserve Notes are needed. In short, if a bank came to the Fed and demanded $20 in cash for its reserves—or, indeed, if it demanded $20 million—all the Fed would have to do is print that amount and pay it out. As we can see, being able to print its own money places the Fed in a uniquely enviable position.

So here we have, at long last, the key to the mystery of the modern inflationary process. It is a process of continually expanding the money supply through continuing Fed purchases of government securities on the open market. Let the Fed wish to increase the money supply by $8 billion, and it will purchase government securities on the open market to a total of $1 billion (if the money multiplier of demand deposits/reserves is 8:1), and the goal will be speedily accomplished. In fact, week after week, even as these lines are being read, the Fed goes into the open market in New York and purchases whatever amount of government bonds it has decided upon, and thereby helps decide upon the amount of monetary inflation."

Murray N. Rothbard, *For a New Liberty* (New York: Macmillan, 1973), pp. 178–182.

Note: In Murray Rothbard's book, first published in 1973, he refers to a 6:1 multiplication factor in the creation of new money. In quoting him, we have changed this ratio to 8:1 to reflect current government standards.

15. Proverbs 29:2.   When the righteous increase, the people rejoice, but when a wicked man rules, people groan.

16. Exodus 23:8.   And you shall not take a bribe, for a bribe blinds the clear-sighted and subverts the cause of the just.

17. Proverbs 16:11.   A just balance and scales belong to the Lord; all the weights of the bag are his concern.

18. Hosea 4:6.   My people are destroyed for the lack of knowledge.

19. Although the Federal Reserve was created by an act of Congress, and its continued operation would not be possible without Congressional approval, for all practical purposes the actions of the Federal Reserve have been unsupervised and unaudited since its inception in 1913.

4

GAMBLING

You said that easy credit causes inflation. I want you to give me an example of how that works.

The rise in real estate costs over the past forty years is a good example of what we're talking about.

Let's say you go looking for a house and find one you like, but the price is $75,000. That's more money than you can afford. It may even be more than you think the house is worth. However, if you can get the money on credit, the price you are willing and able to pay goes up.

If your banker will give you a thirty-year loan, payments will be small. And if you only have to put 20% down, you can buy that $75,000 house for a $15,000 downpayment. On a deal like that, you might be willing to offer $80,000 or $90,000 for the house, particularly if other people are bidding for it too. After all, you expect the value of the house to go up once you have bought it and are living there.

For the past forty years, people have been buying homes on extended credit. Millions of people have benefitted from the process. They bought homes years ago, and their profits have risen greatly. The only problem is that people who want to buy houses now are frozen out of the market. With interest rates running between 12% and 20% a year and the price of a new home starting around $100,000; most people cannot afford mortgage payments.

Thus, certain groups have benefitted from the inflation of real estate, while others have been hurt. One reason inflation is so hard to stop is that so many people have benefitted from it.

What's wrong with that? It's a lot better than being hurt.

Any person who benefits from inflation ALWAYS benefits at someone else's expense.

Over the past twenty years, many Americans have been hurt, some even destroyed financially by inflation.

The effect of this has been to discourage investment and to lower productivity in America. Because of inflation, it is not worth your while to invest in most business projects or to put your money in a bank.

What are you talking about?

If you put a dollar in the bank, after one year you might have $1.05, counting interest. However, because of inflation, the purchasing power of that money is only 95 cents. In two years, it is 89 cents, and in three years, 83 or 84 cents. People who are trying to do the right thing and save their money are actually being ruined every time they deposit a dollar in the bank.

After years of being cheated, people begin to feel foolish saving their money. Then, they do one of three things: they can spend their money because the house, car or clothes they want will be more expensive two or three years from now; they can look for a safer investment, usually nonproductive; or they can speculate with the money.

What do you mean by a nonproductive investment, and what is speculation?

When you lend money to someone who will use it to produce something of value—to open a retail store perhaps, or to design a better engine for cars—your investment results in the production of greater wealth and services for the community at large. In today's economic climate, however, many people are withdrawing their money from productive investments and placing it in nonproductive areas instead—for example, Treasury Bills and U.S. Government Bonds.

Government securities are considered a safe investment because government has the power to tax in order to repay its debts. Yet, they are also *nonproductive*, in that the money government borrows is almost always spent, rather than invested to produce further wealth. The result, in the long run, is that our country becomes poorer. There are fewer goods to buy, and people experience a decline in their standard of living, even if the amount of money they are earning continues to rise.

As for speculation, it's just a fancy word for gambling. You buy some commodity—stock, gold, soybeans, diamonds, or wheat futures—hoping to make a fast profit. You assume that regardless of what you buy, someone else will pay more for it later.

Is there anything wrong with that?

Plenty. For one thing, it is dangerous. Especially if you do not know what you are doing.

Some people become frantic when they realize the effects of inflation. They feel a desperate need to stay ahead of inflation and are willing to gamble for the sake of fast profit.[1] These people are easy marks for "professionals" eager to help them beat inflation with the latest speculative hedge.[2]

"You should invest in beer cans. These are already two years old."

"We're going to find oil here."

"I've got a hot issue for you. This stock is only ten dollars a share right now, but it will be up to fifty within a year."

"The price of real estate is one thing that will never go down."

Emotion, not reason, is the guiding force behind the desire for fast profits. When many people are buying and selling on the commodity markets, all looking for a fast profit, price fluctuations are bound to be extreme.

In this volatile, speculative climate, it is invariably the little man who is wiped out. He does not understand what is happening and is not prepared to deal with price fluctuations as they develop.

Yet, this is only one reason to avoid highly speculative investments. The second reason is a moral one.

> MONEY MAY COME QUICKLY AND EASILY
> WHEN YOU GAMBLE, BUT IT WILL ONLY
> COME AT THE EXPENSE OF SOMEONE ELSE.

SPECULATIVE PROFITS ARE MADE WITHOUT ANYTHING HAVING BEEN PRODUCED. Wealth is simply transferred from one person to the next.

Let's say I don't gamble with my money. What can I do to protect myself against inflation? Which investments are safe?

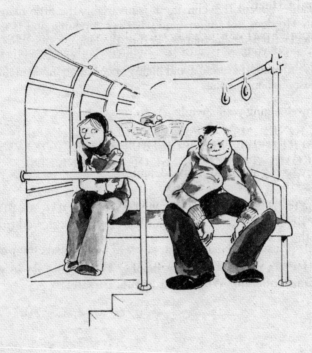

No investment is completely safe. At the present time, fear and emotion rule the marketplace. Trying to decide where the market is going—or where it will be a year from now—is like trying to figure out what a crazy person will do next.[3]

As a result, it's difficult to make money. It's even hard to keep what you have when conditions are so unpredictable. Yet, it is possible for you to gain financial security and avoid the violent fluctuations of today's economy.

How can I do that?

In the second part of this book, we will discuss specific steps you can take to protect yourself against both inflation and depression. For now, you can do your part to stop inflation altogether—

- by changing your spending patterns,

- by not borrowing money for consumption,

- by saving and getting ahead, and

- by achieving financial self-sufficiency.

If you take these immediate steps, you will be resolving the problem of inflation, rather than contributing to its cause.

But I'm just one person. Can my savings really make a difference?

Society is made up of people like you.

Every nation is a collection of individuals. If large numbers of individuals decide to change their spending and savings patterns, they can change society as a whole.

The individual is the unit of society. Society can only be strengthened and changed on the level of the individual. At this time in the history of our nation, we all need to change. Large numbers of individuals thinking and acting correctly can and will change society as a whole.[4]

> ALL OF US ARE RESPONSIBLE FOR CHANGING OUR SOCIETY, AND SOCIETY *WILL CHANGE* IF WE ALL DO OUR SHARE.

NOTES

1. Proverbs 28:20.   A faithful man will abound with blessings, but he who makes haste to be rich will not go unpunished.

2. Proverbs 28:19.   He who tills his land will have plenty of food, but he who follows empty pursuits will have poverty in plenty.

3. James 4:13–14.   Come now, you who say, "Today or tomorrow, we shall go to such and such a city, and spend a year there and engage in business and make a profit."

   Yet you do not know what your life will be like tomorrow. You are just a vapor that appears for a little while and then vanishes away.

4. Proverbs 29:2.   When the righteous increase, the people rejoice.

5

WE, THE PEOPLE...

I think I've figured an easy way out of my financial problems. If I can't afford a house, I'll ask the government for a low-interest loan. And if I can't send my child to college, I think they should pay his tuition. Shouldn't the government help me get what I want?

A lot of people seem to think so. We live in a prosperous country. It is possible for the government to do a lot for its people. For just that reason, some of us have come to believe that the government can do almost anything.

THIS KIND OF THINKING HAS GOTTEN US INTO A LOT OF TROUBLE OVER THE PAST FIFTY YEARS.

How so?

We have allowed ourselves to become weak by relying on government favors. We have gradually forgotten our innate ability to achieve what we want in life.[1]

We have abandoned responsibility for ourselves and have turned to government to solve our problems for us. Now we feel helpless whenever we realize that government is *not* solving our problems. *We feel helpless because we are no longer in control of our lives.*

When the United States was founded almost 200 years ago, Americans did not look to the government to solve their problems. More often than not, they considered government the *source* of their problems, rather than the key to any solution. After all, a government that interfered in people's lives could be used by small but powerful groups to promote their special interests at the expense of everyone else.

Americans had seen this happen before when British colonial policy favored English mercantile interests and the British Crown over the interests of the American people.

Our founding fathers were determined not to let this happen again. Following the Revolutionary War, they saw that some form of government was needed to insure unity among the various states and to ward off any attack by a foreign power. *But to give too much power to a central government was considered dangerous.* Its power could easily be abused and serve to curtail the basic freedom of the American people.[2]

Once, when asked by a friend, "Have you no faith in the men we elect? Have you no confidence in our government?" Thomas Jefferson wrote in reply,

"Confidence is everywhere the parents of despotism . . . . In questions of power, then, let no more be heard of confidence in man, but bind him down from mischief by the chains of the Constitution."

What did Jefferson mean by the "chains of the Constitution"?

He was referring to our form of government, a constitutional republic, which strictly limits the powers of the federal government. Our government is based on a system where voters elect political representatives in order to prevent a few people in power from ever trampling on the rights of the majority. A democracy itself, however, can lead to tyranny and violence if it is not firmly checked.

What do you mean?

Imagine if all the people in your neighborhood got together and voted to seize your house. If you were living in a pure democracy, governed by majority rule, there would be no way for you to protect yourself. You could vote to keep your house, but you could be outnumbered and lose. If you tried to defend your property, you might even be killed!

Whenever a majority rules without regard for the basic rights of others, you have a tyranny as bad as any dictatorship.

I can see that.

Our founding fathers could too. They were afraid a pure democracy would lead to tyranny by the masses. To prevent this from happening in America, the men who drafted our Constitution placed strict limits on majority rule. It was agreed that our government would have certain vital powers, but that it would not be able to overreach these powers unless the Constitution itself were amended. Even amending the Constitution was made a difficult, deliberate process to prevent people from changing the law without careful reflection.[3]

What powers were granted to the federal government by the Constitution?

Government was given the power:

- To borrow money;
- To regulate commerce with foreign nations, between the various states, and with the Indian tribes;
- To establish a uniform rule of naturalization;
- To establish uniform rules on the subject of bankruptcies throughout the United States;
- To coin money and to standardize its value, along with that of foreign coin;
- To fix a standard of weights and measures;
- To punish counterfeiting;
- To establish post offices and postal roads;
- To enact copyright laws;
- To establish lower-level federal courts;
- To handle all foreign affairs;
- To defend the nation by declaring war and by raising and supporting armies and a navy;
- To form a code of law to govern the military;
- To call out the militia to enforce the laws of the land, suppress insurrections, or repel invasions;
- To govern state militias when they serve the national government;
- To prevent any state from erecting barriers to the free flow of goods or people across state lines;
- To admit new states to the Union;
- To govern all territories belonging to the nation which do not have statehood;
- To administer all land belonging to the United States;
- To guarantee that the public acts, records and judicial proceedings of each state are recognized by every other state;
- To guarantee each state a republican form of government; and
- To suggest amendments to the United States Constitution.

These specific activities, which Congress is permitted to finance with your tax money, consist of little more than defending the nation and maintaining smooth relations between the various states. All powers *not* granted to federal government by the Constitution are denied it, as stated in the Bill of Rights:

> The powers not delegated to the United States by the Constitution, nor prohibited by it to the States, are reserved to the States respectively, or to the people. (Amendment X to the United States Constitution, ratified 1791.)

I see the abuses those men were trying to prevent, but why did they have to make the government's powers so fixed and specific? It seems to me that in a changing society, some government power should be flexible.

The men who framed our Constitution recognized the need for flexibility, but they did not want to create a federal government with indefinite powers. Therefore, they solved the problem by establishing our federal system. They created a central government, and then tied it down with detailed specifications of what it could and could not do.

As you have said, there is a need for flexibility in government. When our Constitution was drafted, the flexible powers of government were left with the states. Although some states would undoubtedly misuse their powers on occasion, there were still restraining forces on the power of the states imposed by the federal government. The Constitution granted all free people in the union a common national citizenship and the freedom to travel and trade freely across state lines.

Another restraint on the power of state governments was competition among the states. If any particular state abused its undefined powers, its citizens were free to move to other states. Any abuse in state power could result in the loss of productive citizens and important businesses.

Our founding fathers did not give the federal government unrestricted powers because they did not want to leave any room for the republic to turn into a dictatorship. If the federal government were allowed to make social and political experiments at the discretion of federal officials only, it could become a plundering mechanism—robbing and enslaving the people *under the pretext of taking care of them*. Without the balancing system of the power of the states, there would be no way to restrain or correct any possible tyranny on the part of the federal government. The men who wrote our Constitution took great care to see that this situation could never exist.

Instead, they created a system to govern the United States which was extraordinary. In the balance of power between the federal government and the states, they created a situation where states were free to experiment with social controls and political regulation of business activity without endangering the social liberties of the entire nation.

For 150 years the federal government was limited in scope. To prevent it from being used by any special interest group to exploit other Americans, its size was strictly limited. Government was not permitted to interfere with the daily lives of the American people.

Americans had to fend for themselves. In order to succeed, they had to rely on their own initiative, inner resources, and hard work. Once they had achieved success, however, the fruit of their labor was theirs to enjoy and to use as they saw fit.[4]

There was thus a double incentive working to maintain productivity in America. No one was going to help you if you were capable but unwilling to help yourself. On the other hand, if you were productive, no one was going to take what you had earned and give it to someone else.

If you were successful at transforming your dreams into reality[5]—into a product or service that benefitted other people—you were rewarded financially. The ideal of the American economy was a strong nation with everyone giving and everyone receiving maximum.

This is how the United States was built, how it became the richest nation in the world. Someone with a great idea would work with others to transform that idea into reality.

Until 1913, there was no such thing as income tax or government redistribution of wealth.

What?!! No income tax? How come I've never heard that before?

People tend to forget. *And some people would like you to forget.*[6]

I can see why! Having to pay income tax is like living in chains. You work four or five months a year just to pay your taxes. Who wants that if they can avoid it?

But why was I always told that taxes are inevitable? How did we get along so well in the past without them?

We did not have a large government to support. As for why you were always told that taxes are inevitable, people were describing the reality they knew. If they did not give a part of their income to the government, the Internal Revenue Service would come, seize their home or business, and sell it to pay off their "debt" to the federal government. Under circumstances like those, taxes *are* inevitable. You don't have any choice.

How did we ever allow this to happen?

Surrendering control of our lives to the government was a gradual process. Each step of the way, we were led to believe that the power we were granting government was all for the good. We gradually forgot Thomas Jefferson's warning not to let the government have too much power. Instead of maintaining a limited form of government, the way the Constitution intended, we have given tremendous power to the federal government and to the various agencies it has created.

In 1913 we passed a constitutional amendment allowing a federal income tax. At that time the American people were assured that we would never have to pay more than four or five percent.

In that same year we allowed Congress to sign the Federal Reserve Act into law, with the assurance that it would end the old cycle of economic boom and bust, and thereby create an era of "perpetual prosperity." What the Federal Reserve did, in fact, was grant a handful of bankers virtual control of our nation's money supply. As Congressman Charles A. Lindbergh, Sr. said at the time the bill was passed by Congress:

> This act establishes the most gigantic trust on earth. . . . When the President signs this act the invisible government by the money power, proven to exist by the Money Trust investigation, will be legalized . . . .

> This new law will create inflation whenever the trusts want inflation. . . . From now on depressions will be scientifically created.

In just sixteen years, we had the crash of Wall Street and the biggest depression our country had ever known.

But the Depression was caused by the failure of free enterprise, wasn't it? What does that have to do with the Federal Reserve?

The crash was caused by government intervention in our economy—via the Federal Reserve.

That's not what I've heard. I always thought government intervention was necessary to save capitalism from itself.

Most people were told that in school. And you have to admit, it provides a good justification for government intervention in the economy. The problem is, intervention makes things worse. It doesn't solve problems. It creates them.[7]

How did the Federal Reserve cause the Great Depression?

First, the Federal Reserve inflated our money supply. Between 1921 and 1929, it increased the amount of money in circulation by over sixty percent. Interest rates were kept artificially low, causing a frenzy of speculation in the stock market, where people were encouraged to buy on credit. As a result, stock prices soared until, in 1929, the Federal Reserve's policy of loose money was dramatically reversed. A collapse soon followed, ushering in the Great Depression of the 1930's, during which our money supply actually shrank by thirty-three percent.

After the collapse, there was a tremendous amount of suffering. Our economy had been severely disrupted, and the American people demanded a change of leadership in government. In 1932, Franklin D. Roosevelt was elected President of the United States. He had run on a Democratic platform which promised, among other things:

- a drastic reduction in government spending,
- a balanced federal budget, and
- the removal of all government interference in the private economy.[8]

This is what the American people were instinctively demanding when they elected FDR in 1932. Once in office, however, Roosevelt did exactly the opposite of what he had promised. Rather than allowing the country to get back on its feet by returning to the free market system, he declared that the federal government should solve the nation's problems. Only, to do this, he needed power.

What kind of power?

The power to regulate all aspects of our economy.

How did he get people to go along with that?

He said he would solve their problems. That was a tempting offer in the middle of the Great Depression.

Is that what the New Deal was all about?

That's right. FDR persuaded America to adopt a new philosophy of government and called it the New Deal. It was a philosophy that had been around Europe for a number of years. Only there it was called socialism. The idea behind this philosophy was simple: whenever there is a problem in society, the government should step in and solve it.

Is that necessarily wrong?

It's fine for a government to solve problems as long as it does not create newer and bigger ones in the process. Our Constitution provides state governments with broad powers so that they can experiment with social change. However, it prohibits experimentation on a *national* level, where everyone will be affected if the experiment gets out of hand.

That makes sense.

During the Depression when millions of people were starving, it was necessary for someone to feed them.[9] But not all the problems we face are so basic. And not all solutions are so simple or obvious.

Once the Depression was over, following World War II, the philosophy of government intervention was not discarded. It was embraced all the more strongly on the *federal* level.

191

People had a taste of what government can do for them. They had seen how "easy" it can make their lives.

This is the essence of socialism: the individual hands responsibility for his or her life over to government. The government then becomes the main source of wealth and power in society. Individual freedom is gradually lost in exchange for collective "security."

How is individual freedom lost?

Government starts telling you what to do, how to live your life, how to run your business. Obviously, the more power is gathered in government hands, the less remains with you.

In one sense. But ultimately, *I* control the government. After all, we live in a democracy.

Don't you remember what we said about democracy before? It's true that you have a vote. But if everyone else decides to take your property, there is not much you can do about it.

Unfortunately, this is exactly what's been happening in America. The old safeguards of individual freedom, which were built into our Constitution, have gradually been broken down—always in the name of social or economic justice.

We seldom pause to ask whether what the government does is constitutional. OFTEN IT IS NOT. But that does not matter to most of us since we benefit from the government's actions in the short run.

We hate to pay taxes, but most of us love free gifts. When we receive unemployment compensation, a low-interest student loan, or a crop subsidy, we don't ask where the money came from. We're just happy to get it.

AS TIME HAS PASSED, MORE AND MORE AMERICANS HAVE COME TO EXPECT GOVERNMENT TO USE ITS POWER FOR THEIR BENEFIT.

After all, the government can do anything. It can build bridges, roads, hospitals and schools. It can distribute food and jobs.

192

We all line up to receive government handouts.[10]

There doesn't seem to be any end to it. The line keeps getting longer year after year . . .

after year.[11]

Whenever we want something, whether it is price supports for tobacco or greater social security benefits, we write to our Congressman and tell him what we want. We even threaten not to vote for him if he doesn't give it to us.

I guess we do.

Maybe your Congressman will get that big water project you want approved, or the loan for your daughter to go to college. But it is important for you to recognize that government cannot produce these things out of thin air. It can tax. It can borrow. It can put cash into your pocket. But real goods and services will only be provided if someone has actually produced them.[12]

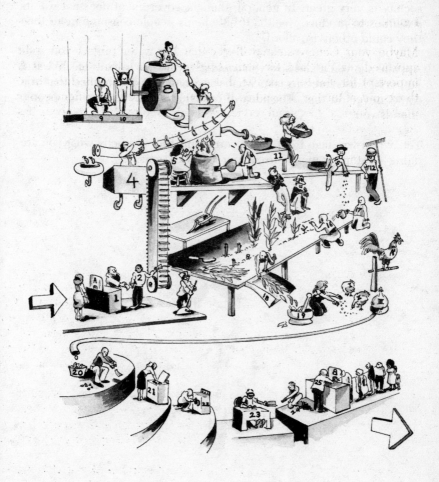

Government simply transfers what has already been produced—and not very efficiently at that.

But doesn't government produce some things that nobody else would?

There are some projects too large and expensive to be undertaken by individuals or private corporations, even though the return they offer society is very great. In general, though, government does not use its revenues to produce wealth. It only helps people consume more than they could otherwise afford.

A while ago you asked how you could get what you want in life. We said you could use force to take what you want, but you replied that you could never do that. The idea of extorting money from other people offends you.

Yet, when you take from the government, that is exactly what you are doing—extorting money from your fellow citizens.

What do you mean?

The government does not produce the things it gives to you. It only transfers their ownership to you after having taken them from someone else.

You would never consider going to someone's house in the middle of the night with a gun, saying:

"I'm your neighbor from down the street. Give me your money because I need it more than you do."

And yet you say you might write your Congressman for help in buying a new house or sending your son to college.

I'm not sure if I would at this point.

After all, it's easy to take from a faceless entity. You don't see the **people** you are hurting.

But if you realize the government is only an intermediary and that you are, in fact, robbing your neighbor from down the street, across the state, or *wherever* taxpayers live . . .

you might not want to do it.

But it sounds like you're against all taxes. That can't be right.

As we have said before, some government services are vital. Some tax must be levied to finance these essential programs. Government should not, however, be made to serve special interest groups. After all, why should you be taxed to pay for government tea tasters, or to keep the price of milk high when almost everyone wants to see it lower? Why should your tax money be used to insure small fishing boats? The government doesn't insure *your* car.

But if you cut taxes, aren't you being a Robin Hood in reverse, taking from the poor to give to the rich?

This may come as a surprise to you, but most people who receive money from the government are not poor, or members of a minority group. They belong to the middle or upper-class. Maybe they are businessmen, receiving subsidies in the form of government contracts or export loans. Maybe they have a job with the government, filling out forms, inventing new regulations, and expanding the power of the federal bureaucracy. Maybe they receive an inflated government pension. Or maybe they work for a company that is being propped up by the federal government, protected against bankruptcy and foreign competition. Regardless, these are the people who benefit most from government spending, not the people that you call "poor."

By cutting taxes, you allow hard-working people to keep more of the money they earn. You are not giving them anything.

Wait a minute! I pay my taxes! Why shouldn't I get something back from government?

You should, if the point of taxation were to make a fair exchange with the government—if your tax dollars were meant to provide you with certain specific services in return. But that is not the point of taxation in America today. Your money is not meant to be returned to you.

Under a limited form of government, you could expect to pay a small tax each year. In return, government would provide for the national defense, the maintenance of law and order, roads, and perhaps a few other things. For the rest, you would have to fend for yourself.

The reason taxes are so high today is that everyone is demanding favors from the government. To provide these services, the government must raise taxes. It must take money from you in order to give it to someone else. Government has become a plundering mechanism, with everyone trying to manipulate it for their own benefit.

Many of us long to fill our pockets with government subsidies. We bribe politicians. We write threatening letters to our Congressmen. We form special interest groups with full-time lobbyists in Washington.[13] Corporate executives demand import quotas and government support so they can avoid bankruptcy and remain in business. Farmers demand price supports and special water projects. Labor leaders expect greater benefits for their rank and file, while minorities demand special treatment from the government.

We have a situation today where everyone is robbing everyone else!

In the final analysis, though, we must all foot the bill. We must all pay the cost of government inefficiency by supporting a huge bureaucracy, whose job it is to redistribute the wealth that is taken from us each year.

We're all in the same boat—secretaries, teachers, mechanics, lawyers, factory workers—you name it. We all pay taxes that are too high.

NOTES

1. Philippians 4:13.   I can do all things through Him who strengthens me.

2. Isaiah 33:22.   For the Lord is our judge, the Lord is our lawgiver, the Lord is our king.

3. Proverbs 22:28.   Do not move the ancient boundary which your fathers have set.

4. Ecclesiastes 5:19.   Furthermore, as for every man to whom God has given riches and wealth, He has also empowered him to eat from them and to receive his reward and rejoice in his labor; this is the gift of God.

5. Proverbs 13:12.   Desire fulfilled is a tree of life.

6. Deuteronomy 8:18.   But you shall remember the Lord your God, for it is He who is giving you power to make wealth.

7. Various scholars have demonstrated how government intervention in the economy both causes and prolongs depressions. See Murray N. Rothbard, *America's Great Depression* (Princeton, New Jersey: D. Van Nostrand, 1963) and Percy L. Greaves, Jr., *Understanding the Dollar Crisis* (Belmont, Massachusetts: Western Islands, 1973).

8. To quote Roosevelt himself, from a radio speech he delivered on March 2, 1930:

    > Under the 18th Amendment Congress has been given the right to legislate on this particular subject (liquor), but this is not the case in the matter of a great number of other vital problems of government, such as the conduct of public utilities, of banks, of insurance, of business, of agriculture, of education, of social welfare and of a dozen other features. In these, Washington must not be encouraged to interfere.

9. Isaiah 58:7.   Is it not to divide your bread with the hungry, and bring the homeless poor into the house; when you see the naked, to cover him; and not to hide yourself from your own flesh?

10. Second Thessalonians 3:8.   Nor did we eat anyone's bread without paying for it, but with labor and hardship we kept working night and day so that we might not be a burden to any of you.

11. Proverbs 12:27.   The precious possession of a man is diligence.

12. Proverbs 10:4.   Poor is he who works with a negligent hand, but the hand of the diligent makes rich.

13. Deuteronomy 16:19.   You shall not distort justice; you shall not be partial, and you shall not take a bribe, for a bribe blinds the eyes of the wise and perverts the words of the righteous.

6

THE PARTY IS OVER

Wait a minute. There are some people in this country who are much wealthier than others. Don't you think they should pay higher taxes to balance things out?

Let's use the example of a person who develops a new form of technology which saves other people millions of dollars in heating costs every year. He may become a millionaire, but it will not be at the expense of anyone else. If he becomes wealthy, it will be because he has given to others, and the marketplace has come to recognize and reward his contribution.

High taxes penalize anyone who contributes greatly to society. Imposing heavy taxes on them in order to finance programs which benefit others without generating greater wealth for society as a whole is counterproductive. You force those who are already contributing to society to give twice, while encouraging others to take it easy and not give anything at all.

But what about hunger? Would you let people starve?

We don't want people to starve, but government can't afford to support people who truly are able to take care of themselves. It would be much more productive for the nation and more fulfilling for these people psychologically to do some kind of work. That would get both sides off the hook in the long run.

If the social system encourages people to be weak, that's unfair to the people receiving aid, as well as being harmful to society as a whole. What we want to do is eliminate the *cause* of the problem, not just the symptom. We need to encourage people to be self-sufficient and to make the most of their lives.

You're right. Keeping people dependent all their lives is no solution at all. But what should we do?

The secret is finding work you enjoy. When you enjoy your work, it's easy for you to put a lot of thought and energy into it. You become very productive, and your work becomes a form of giving. Once you find work you enjoy and which meets a valid need in society, you will be on the path to getting what you want in life without having to take anything from anyone else. There is, however, a price you will have to pay.

210

I knew there was a catch. What is the price?

You will have to give up your weakness and lack of self-confidence—and stop looking to government for help.

That's not so bad.

No. In fact, it's good. Right now we *have* to change because . . .

The party is over.

What party? What are you talking about?

The orgy of government spending we've had for the past fifty years. The party of government giving people almost anything they want.

You mean people who depend on government will have to stop? Will they have to take care of themselves?

If we want to avoid severe economic problems, they will. Some people may not want to stop depending on the government for favors, but before long, they may not have any choice. The government cannot afford to continue giving so much to so many people without causing a disaster. If that happens, the people hurt most will be those who have forgotten how to take care of themselves, how to think for themselves, and how to use their own creativity to get what they want out of life.

You're always talking about some kind of catastrophe. What I want to know is, if things have been going on like this for so many years, why can't they just continue? Why does the party have to stop?

You have asked a very important question.

The road we have been on leads to disaster. It's a long road. When we first got on it many years ago, we were free to travel without facing immediate danger. But the end of the road is now in sight. If we do not change direction soon, we will go right over the edge.

That's a good analogy, but what are you really talking about? What have we been doing all these years that is so wrong?

We have lived high on the hog without wanting to pay the bill. Instead of working to earn the standard of living we want to enjoy, we have taken the easy way out, through consumer credit and government subsidies. We have encouraged politicians to give us the wealth of others who are more productive than we are and have justified our demands by saying that we are entitled to all these benefits just because we live in America.[1]

In order to transfer such large sums of wealth, millions of government employees had to be hired. It was a gradual process, but now one out of every two Americans depends on the government for some kind of support.

Twenty million Americans are directly employed by federal, state and local governments.

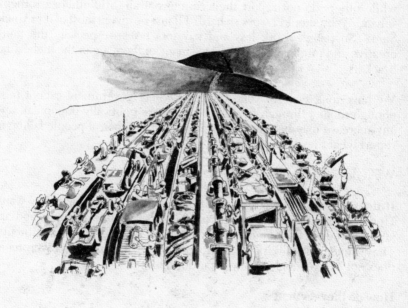

Many millions more provide the government with goods and services.

As if that were not enough, thousands more are involved in the process of collecting, or fighting the collection of government taxes. Tax avoidance has become a major industry in America. Some of the most brilliant people in this country spend their entire working lives creating new tax laws or devising intricate schemes to avoid tax liability for their clients. Yet, despite the time, energy, and money they spend, NOTHING IS PRODUCED!

When fewer people work productively, the burden grows heavier on those who do. This causes some people to cheat on their tax returns, while others do not report their earnings at all. Still others ask themselves, "Why should I work so hard? I'll just be giving most of it to Uncle Sam." So people work less and pay less taxes—especially the more creative and intelligent people since many of them are in the highest tax brackets.

We have long since reached the point where government cannot raise enough money through taxes. New taxes are politically unpopular, and any increase may be offset by an increased number of people failing to report what they have earned.

What does the government do then?

It does not have enough money to give people everything they want. However, politicians are supported by special interest groups and are afraid to reduce the number of favors they provide for their constituents. They fund politically popular programs even though the government does not have enough money to pay for them.

How do they do that?

THEY BORROW MONEY.

Is there anything wrong with the government borrowing money?

For a long time it was not a serious problem because the government borrowed such small amounts. By now, though, it is borrowing billions of dollars each week. The government is taking savings which would otherwise be channeled into productive investments, and is spending this money on consumer goods to increase people's current standard of living. Money that is borrowed by the government is not used to produce new wealth. It is used to buy goods and services which are already in limited supply, driving prices even higher.

How much money does the government borrow?

Right now, the government is borrowing more than half of all new savings in America—over $100 billion dollars a year. In the 1960's the government borrowed only 4% of all new savings. This figure rose to 25% during the 1970's. By now, the government consumes more than 50% of all the money which is available for investment in this country.

BY DRAINING THE MARKET OF CAPITAL THAT WOULD OTHERWISE BE USED FOR INVESTMENT, THE GOVERNMENT CAUSES A DECREASE IN THE NUMBER OF NEW JOBS, A FALL IN PRODUCTIVITY, AND A LONG-TERM DECLINE IN THE NATION'S STANDARD OF LIVING.

Money to new businesses is choked off, and the economy can't grow.

What is the short-term effect of government borrowing?

High interest rates. Since government borrows a large portion of the money that is available, this makes the cost of borrowing high for everyone. Many businesses and consumers are in debt and have no choice but to pay the higher interest rates, even if they cannot afford them. As a result, many people are driven bankrupt; the economy is hurt; and profits decline even further, forcing businesses to lay off people and making it difficult for them to give their employees raises or promotions.

We are mortgaging our future . . .

in order to enjoy life a little bit more today.

Aren't there any limits to how much the government can borrow?

Unlike private individuals, the government has an almost endless source of revenue. It has the power to tax, and thereby confiscate the wealth of its people to repay its debts.

This makes default on government debts seem much less likely than bankruptcy on the part of an individual or corporation. It encourages people to lend money to the government, even though no one would lend money to an individual acting that way. However, government bankruptcy is not impossible. Some people, in fact, are beginning to question whether the government will ever repay all its loans. The official debt is well over one trillion dollars, and hidden liabilities, such as social security and federal pensions ($7.3 trillion) are even greater than those officially acknowledged.

INFLATION IS ALREADY CAUSING A PARTIAL DEFAULT, AS IT MAKES DEBTS CHEAPER TO REPAY.

If enough people ever doubt the government's intention or ability to repay all of its loans, there could be a sudden panic out of government IOU's. People would try to get rid of Treasury Bills, Government Bonds, and U.S. dollar bills as fast as possible, exchanging them for anything of intrinsic value. In other words, we could have sudden, runaway inflation.

When an individual goes bankrupt, only a few people are affected. However, a government bankruptcy would affect everyone. It would drown the entire nation in worthless IOU's, and millions of people would lose everything they own.

Do you really think that could happen?

Yes, we do. Thousands of businesses go bankrupt every year because they spend more money than they take in. For the past fifty years, federal spending has been so great that only rarely has the government been able to meet all of its financial needs through taxes. Sometimes it cannot even borrow as much money as it would like to spend. To cover the difference, the government *creates* as much money as it needs.

Are you kidding?

The only legal money in America today is the Federal Reserve Note, and the Federal Reserve has a monopoly on its printing.

If the government wants to spend more money than it has available through taxes or borrowing, it can sell debt to the Federal Reserve, which will credit the government's account and issue it money to spend. This is called double entry bookkeeping, otherwise known as monetization of the federal debt. Money is created out of thin air and put into circulation, as if it were the real thing.

"I'm a computer operator. I used to be bored at my old job.

"Then I saw an ad in the paper to work with the Federal Reserve. It said I could put a lot of fun into my life.

"Now my life is wonderful! Every time I push a button, I create a million dollars out of thin air.

227

"The only problem is they're making me push that button all day long. I'm getting a terrible pain in my finger."

What are the results of this increase in the supply of money?

People who receive the money are receiving Federal Reserve Notes which are identical to those held by everyone else in the country. They are able to go out and buy anything they want with the money government gives them. But since there is more money in circulation and no new goods have been produced, prices rise. The value of everyone else's money goes down.

This is how inflation works. Inflation is a *hidden tax*—an increase in the supply of money which causes the value of money to go down. Only the first person to spend the new money—in this case, the government—is able to buy things at their old price. Everyone else is hurt.

I never knew any of this before. It's outrageous! I can't believe what the government is doing to us.

More accurately, THIS IS WHAT WE ARE DOING TO OURSELVES.

What do you mean?

Inflation has two primary causes—the expansion of credit and massive increases in our money supply. Both are products of government policies, and both are subject to government control. However, the federal government simply acts on behalf of its citizens, which in realistic terms means whoever controls Congress. That is why *we* need to regain control of the government and take that power away from the special interest groups which control it now. GOVERNMENT SPENDING CAN BE CONTROLLED, BUT ONLY IF THE AMERICAN PEOPLE DEMAND THAT THIS BE DONE.

You mean it is my responsibility?

That's right. For fifty years now people have been demanding easy credit and countless favors from government, making high taxes, inflation, and a steadily growing national debt all but inevitable. We have followed inflationary policies whose short-term benefits were obvious, but whose long-term, negative consequences were difficult to perceive. By now, though, the future is upon us. The effects of fifty years of inflationary government policy can be seen in the decline of American productivity and the fragmentation of American politics into thousands of special interest groups, each vying for a larger piece of a shrinking national pie.

What does this all add up to?

It adds up to a huge problem. We have created a monster out of years of reckless spending. It now threatens to destroy us.

The purpose of investment is to produce more goods, *not* to forgo consumption altogether. The government defeats this purpose by consuming so much of our capital now, leaving far less than we need to invest in the future.

This creates unemployment.

An employer might want to hire people, but if he doesn't have any money, how is he going to do it?

On the other hand, if people were saving, there would be money available for business loans and other productive investments.

Then there would be more jobs and more products available for everyone.

High taxes, government spending, and consumer debt all put money to nonproductive use. As a result, many productive investments are never made. Good business ideas are available, but it is difficult to translate them into reality with the situation the way it is today.

IN ORDER FOR THINGS TO GET BETTER, WE MUST TELL THE GOVERNMENT TO CHANGE. ALSO, WE OURSELVES MUST CHANGE.

We must refuse to travel any longer on a road which leads to disaster, even if it seems to be paved with gold.[2]

NOTES

1. Second Thessalonians 3:10.   For even when we were with you, we used to give you this order: if anyone will not work, neither let him eat.

2. Proverbs 4:14.   Do not enter the path of the wicked, and do not proceed in the way of evil men.

   Job 18:10.   A noose for him is hid in the ground, and a trap for him on the path.

7

THE THREE PATHS

This is serious. Things seem to be getting out of control.

They are.

Right now, we are headed for disaster.

What kind of disaster?

We could have hyperinflation, deflation, or a brief but painful depression as inefficient businesses are forced into bankruptcy.

What does hyperinflation mean?

Hyperinflation is a situation where prices are going up every week or even every day.

If that happens, a loaf of bread could soon cost $100 and a meal in a restaurant over $1,000. A complete breakdown of the economy would not be long in coming. When no one trusts a nation's currency, everyone is forced to barter. Production and trade become difficult, if not impossible.

Can you imagine going into a food store and saying, "I'll trade you my spare tire for all this food. It's brand new."

Or how about pulling into a gas station and saying, "I'll trade you my toaster for a tankful of gas."

At that rate, it wouldn't take long for trade to reach a standstill.

That's awful. Would deflation be any better?

At first glance it seems to be. During a deflation, the supply of money *contracts* instead of expanding. Prices go down because there is less money in circulation.

How does that make prices decline?

If people have less money, they cannot afford to pay high prices or to buy as much as they did before. The demand for goods and services becomes less, and prices have to fall.

Another result of a deflation is that many businesses are unable to pay their debts. When they become frantic for cash, they cut prices even further to meet their financial needs.

This presents a problem for many individuals as well. Think of all the homeowners and people making payments on cars. With less money in circulation, they would find it harder to pay their debts. Those who were overextended in debt and could not get their hands on sufficient cash to make their monthly payments would go bankrupt.

THEY WOULD LOSE EVERYTHING THEY OWN.

This is what happened in 1929. We had a huge deflationary depression.

What about the brief depression you mentioned earlier?

There are many inefficient companies in America today being propped up by government subsidies and inflationary credit. If we stop inflating the money supply and cut back on government subsidies, a brief depression could result as these inefficient companies are forced to improve their performance or go out of business.

Would that be bad?

It would be painful for a while since many people would lose their old jobs and have to find new work. But it would be far better than trying to run away from the problem by printing more money and experiencing hyperinflation as a result.

Why is that?

A depression would end quickly if the government refused to intervene in the economy. It would be like letting the air out of a balloon that's been blown way up. Once the air was released, the tension would be gone.

Hyperinflation, on the other hand, means expanding the balloon until it finally explodes. During a runaway inflation, people lose all confidence in paper money. Then you have a real problem on your hands because your economy has been destroyed.

Is one of these situations inevitable?

We don't think so, although . . .

Some people are predicting total disaster. They feel we will continue on our present course and plunge straight into a full-scale economic collapse.

Why do they feel disaster is inevitable?

As they see it, not enough Americans understand the nature and the gravity of our economic problems. What's more, they doubt that many Americans, even if they did understand the problem, would be willing to take the necessary steps to avert the danger.

That's not giving us much credit.

No, it's not. But you should understand that we are already in *grave* danger. If we want to avoid disaster, a majority of Americans will have to undergo a huge change of attitude and behavior. We will have to make considerable sacrifices in the short run. And we must act NOW!

I'm not going to sit by and let this country go down the drain.

It's encouraging to hear you say that. After all, disaster is *not* inevitable. Runaway inflation and depression are not the only possibilities that lie before us.

There is a third path we can take, a path which will lead to great prosperity—if we are willing to face up to our problems and do what is necessary to solve them.

We must put our faith in God and return to His ways.[1]

One thing is certain, however. If we continue on the path we have travelled for the past fifty years, consuming more than we produce and printing money to finance that consumption, hyperinflation *will* be the inevitable result.

Most of us fear the prospect of economic hardship, even when it promises to be temporary. We seldom realize that economic pain can serve as a warning signal, letting us know that something is wrong before it gets out of hand. Corporate bankruptcies and widespread unemployment tell us that something is wrong with our economy. If we listen to these signs instead of merely bandaging the wound with additional government aid, we can avert much more serious problems in the future.

Take one example: an old business that is no longer productive. When profits decline, the message is clear. Management should adjust to the changing demands of the market and help workers retrain to perform jobs more essential in today's economy.

Of course, both workers and management can demand government aid. This will not change the economic reality, however. The government may intervene to relieve their suffering, but it cannot make a poorly run company more efficient. Its intervention will, in fact, reward inefficiency by relieving the company of any need to change.

While temporary solutions may work in the short run, the long-range consequences of ignoring the warning signal will be much more painful than what we are trying to avoid now.

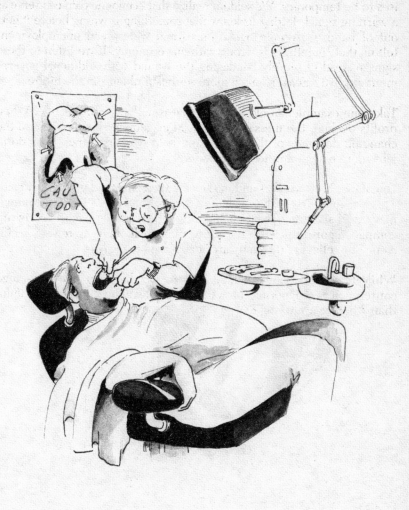

"I'm afraid we'll have to pull this tooth. It's badly infected."

"I'd rather you left the tooth alone. How about giving me some pills to kill the pain instead?"

"If I did that, I wouldn't be doing my job. I can give you some pills to eliminate your pain for a while, but three or four months from now, when the pills no longer work, I'm still going to have to pull the tooth. By then, however, the infection may have spread throughout your body."

Whether you have a toothache or a job that is no longer in demand, you can avoid your day of reckoning for a while. If you belong to a union, you can keep your old job by preventing your company from adopting technological innovations. Or if your company is going out of business, you can ask the government to set up tariffs and import quotas, or even lend money to your company so that you still get a paycheck. However, none of this will solve the real problem. Your company will not become any more competitive, nor will you become any more productive. You'll just be getting a welfare check from the government, written at taxpayers' expense. Even if the government does step in and try to solve your problems, whatever help it offers can only be temporary.

Why is that?

As long as a nation is wealthy, its government can afford to subsidize some businesses and some individuals. If too many of its industries become inefficient, however, and too many people unproductive, that country will no longer be rich. There will not be enough people producing wealth to support everyone else.

The only way the government can subsidize some people is by taxing those who are hard-working and efficient. High taxes eventually backfire, though. They create a vicious cycle, reducing everyone's incentive to produce. Eventually, the problem can become so widespread that the government is no longer able to support everyone who needs help. If there are too many people without jobs, too many failing corporations, and too many insolvent banks, the government will not be able to save everyone.

Are you sure?

Any business that loses money year after year must eventually go bankrupt. The same is true of the government. It can't support too many inefficient corporations, unemployed workers, and government bureaucrats without going bankrupt itself, although the steps leading to its collapse would be gradual and involved.

You mean our government could go bankrupt, just like Braniff or Penn Central?

That's right.

It's hard to believe. Are we anywhere close to that happening?

We are far too close for comfort. Already the government does not have enough money to meet its financial obligations. As a result, it has been borrowing money to finance its deficit spending. We have now reached a point where interest payments alone are the third largest item in the federal budget—over 100 billion dollars a year!

Numbers like that don't mean much to me.

Can you imagine if your neighbor was so far in debt that after food and rent his next biggest expense was interest payments? Our government is in a similar position today.

THE OFFICIAL DEBT OF THE UNITED STATES GOVERN-
MENT IS OVER ONE TRILLION DOLLARS, WITH MORE THAN
TEN TRILLION DOLLARS IN ADDITIONAL UNFUNDED
LIABILITIES.

And right now Uncle Sam is only making payments on the *interest*.

**That's impossible! Nobody can owe that much money. Our nation must
be drowning in debt.**

It is.

Our situation is so precarious that a single accident could trigger the onset of hyperinflation. There are many timebombs ticking away in our economy . . .

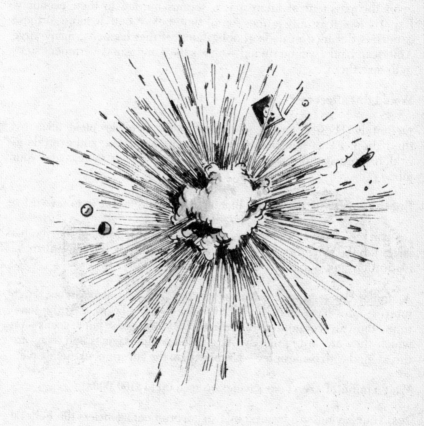

any one of which could explode and bring on disaster.

Time bombs? What are you talking about?

To give you an example, many major American banks have lent billions of dollars to Third World nations—nations which, for all practical purposes, are unable to repay their loans. For many of these countries, even the payment of interest is a serious burden to their economy. Experts feel it is only a question of time before one or more of these countries defaults on its loan obligations. If that happens, many large American banks will be ruined—unless the American government steps in to save them.

Would this affect me?

Definitely. These defaults could set off a chain of bankruptcies all across the nation. Financially vulnerable corporations, banks, and even debt-ridden municipalities could fall. You might lose your savings and your job.

But the government won't let that happen. It has to step in to save us!

It's hard to say what the government will do. The problem may be too large for the government to handle. Banks are not the only financial institutions in trouble.

A similar danger threatens many savings and loan associations. High interest rates have made it expensive for them to borrow. At the same time, they are committed to low-interest, thirty-year home loans—on which they are losing money. As a result, many savings and loans are threatened with bankruptcy—far more than the government can handle.

Wait a minute! Aren't our savings insured up to $100,000?

Yes, your savings are insured by two government agencies, the Federal Deposit Insurance Corporation (FDIC) and the Federal Savings and Loan Insurance Corporation (FSLIC). The only problem is that for every one hundred dollars of potential liability, the FDIC has less than eighty cents in reserve. It can bail out a few banks, but if there is widespread trouble, the FDIC will run out of money.

What?!!

This is an outrage! How can the government be so irresponsible? How could it do this to me?

Banks don't want people to know how much trouble they are in, so the federal government helps them out. The FDIC, rather than ensuring that banks will follow sound lending practices, participates in a cover-up, allowing things to continue unchanged.[2]

This is no different, however, from what the government is doing when it gives your son a college loan. It wants him to have a good education, but it forgets that someone else must pay for it. The same is true of subsidies to peanut farmers, milk producers, and the American Merchant Marine. They all come from the taxpayer's pocket.

How did things ever get to be this way? I never said I wanted government to support peanut or tobacco farmers.

No, you just requested subsidies for yourself. The problem is everyone else did too.

OVER THE PAST FIFTY YEARS, MORE AND MORE OF US HAVE BEGUN USING GOVERNMENT TO PROMOTE OUR OWN SPECIAL INTERESTS. BY NOW, ALMOST EVERYONE IS TRYING TO TAKE ADVANTAGE OF EVERYONE ELSE, THROUGH GOVERNMENT.[3]

No wonder we have so many problems.

We all look at the short term—what we can get right now. We don't consider the effect of our actions on everyone else, or even on ourselves and our future.[4] We rationalize the subsidies we receive from government by saying, "I'm not going to bankrupt the government by getting a low-interest loan for a new house." The head of a corporation will say, "This is a rich country. The government can afford to bail us out."

One more home or business bail-out is not significant in itself, but sooner or later there must be a straw that breaks the camel's back. We don't know when that will be, and we certainly do not want to find out.

What about my financial security, though? What if some banks do collapse?

You will scream and so will everyone else. That means the government will be under tremendous pressure to intervene and prevent you from losing your savings. It probably would, but the only way it could do this would be by printing billions of dollars and distributing that money to people whose savings would otherwise be lost.

Wouldn't that be better than all of us losing our money?

We don't know. It could trigger hyperinflation. People are already suspicious. They don't trust the government or paper money. That is why inflation hedges—such as real estate, precious gems, and gold—became so popular over the last decade. That is why the price of gold rose from $35 to over $800 an ounce during the 1970's.

ANY DECISION TO PUMP LARGE AMOUNTS OF MONEY INTO THE ECONOMY, FOR WHATEVER REASON, WOULD VASTLY ACCELERATE THE PROCESS OF HYPERINFLATION.

Right now, people are waiting to see what will happen. They want to know if the government is determined to end inflation. If it does abandon its inflationary policies, people will gradually regain confidence in the dollar. On the other hand, if these policies are not reversed, inflation will continue unchecked as the American people lose further confidence in themselves, in their currency, and in their government.

The way we are going, even without a series of bank failures or corporate bankruptcies, we could soon experience the kind of inflation that overtook Germany after World War I.

At that time, money was being printed so fast and prices were rising so quickly that people had to be paid every day. When they were paid, they were given half an hour off from work, and they would run to the store with a wheelbarrow full of money to buy whatever they could before prices rose even higher.

The currency soon became worthless. People lost all confidence in their money—and in their government. They lost confidence in democracy and began looking for a strong leader. We all know what happened next. Adolf Hitler rose to power on a wave of frustration, anger, and resentment over the troubles which had beset Germany.

Surely that could never happen in America.

On the contrary. Prices are already rising every few weeks or months at the store. Many people spend their entire paycheck before prices can get even higher. We have not entered hyperinflation yet, but we are well on our way.

But all this talk about Hitler? What does that have to do with us?

When people encounter difficulties, they can respond in one of two ways. They can view the problem as a challenge and seek to overcome it, or they can feel victimized, persecuted, helpless—and look for someone who promises to solve their problems for them.

Many people in America already look to the government to solve their problems instead of relying on themselves for support. By surrendering control over their lives, they encourage the growth of an omnipotent government.

We don't know what would emerge from the ruins of an actual collapse. But we do know that there could be widespread poverty, violence, and chaos.[5]

Under conditions like these, people would be desperate. Many would do anything, or sacrifice anything, to restore order to society. Individual freedom and democracy might be the first things to go . . .

as a new "leader" emerged to guide the nation out of chaos.

Are you sure that could happen in America?

If you didn't have a job or enough money to buy food for yourself and your family, what would you do? You'd have only two alternatives. You could either solve the problem yourself or let someone else solve it for you.

Now if a politician came along and said he needed emergency powers to end the nation's crisis, and if he promised you a job and money, would you be interested?

I guess I would. That sounds like a fair deal to me, especially if those emergency powers were only temporary.

Do you really believe they would be? A man who seizes power during a crisis is like a magician. He has to fool people in order to perform his trick. He doesn't really want to solve your problems or ours. In fact, *he can't solve them. That is something we must do for ourselves.* What the politician really wants is power. So like a magician performing his trick, he distracts us. He gets us to shift our attention to the breakdown of law and order, and while we're distracted, he performs his trick in a way that we hardly even notice.

What the "Magician" doesn't want you to see is that he is gaining control of your life. If he said he wanted to become a dictator, nobody would support him. Instead, he shifts our attention to the fact that we have a problem. He claims he can solve our problem, if only we will give him the authority to do so.

What does that mean? What authority?

It means we're supposed to let him do whatever he thinks is necessary to solve our problems for us. We're supposed to put the law in his hands. As history proves, however, once you give someone that kind of power, it is very hard to get it back.

What kind of powers are you talking about?

To give you one example, wage and price controls.

I think the price of some things is getting out of hand. Personally, the idea of government keeping prices down doesn't bother me. My daughter just had her first baby. She says the price of milk is outrageous. Don't you think something as basic as milk should be priced within everyone's reach?

Of course it should. But in dealing with the problem, you have to be realistic and locate its exact cause.

What is that?

Rising prices are caused by inflation—
that is, by increasing our money supply.
The answer to the problem then
is very simple. You control prices by
stopping inflation—by preventing the
government and banks from increasing
the money supply.

Wage and price controls distract your
attention from the real cause of rising
prices. They simply concentrate more
power in the hands of government without
solving the basic problem. The price of milk,
or any of our basic necessities, would be
within reach if inflation were controlled.

The real solution to all of these problems
is to eliminate inflation—which can be done
if the American people demand it.

When Thomas Jefferson warned, "The price of liberty is eternal vigilance,"[6] he knew what he was talking about. So did Edmund Burke, when he said, "The only thing necessary for the triumph of evil is for good men to do nothing."[7]

An economic crisis in America could set the stage for a loss of freedom and the growth of a totalitarian government. For this reason, if for no other, we want to avoid it.

What if there is one, though?

Then we will have to be even more careful to ensure that our way of life is not destroyed. We will have to take responsibility for ourselves, our friends, and our family, and come through the crisis on our own, rather than giving the government powers which it could easily abuse.

Do you think we'll avoid a crisis, or is it probably too late?

Hyperinflation is not inevitable. It comes from following a specific policy—from increasing the money supply. Policies can be changed.

Maybe I should write my Congressman.

That would be an excellent idea.

What should I say, though? If we can't keep inflating, what should we do?

We must avoid further inflation, yet we must also be careful when cutting back.

If you suddenly realize you are headed towards a cliff at 80 miles per hour, you have to stop. That's obvious. Yet, you don't want to panic, hit the brakes, and stop so quickly that you injure yourself in the process.

It is much easier to adapt to change when change is gradual. If we stop inflation by slamming on the brakes—decreasing the money supply and cutting government spending to the bone—a deflationary collapse will occur. Businesses heavily in debt will go bankrupt, unemployment will soar, and there will be tremendous dislocation as millions of workers are forced to look for new jobs. We could have a depression like that of the 1930's, and we don't want that to happen again.

Then what should we do?

WE MUST ENCOURAGE GOVERNMENT TO INITIATE BALANCED CHANGE, WHICH WILL RESULT IN THE CREATION OF A SOUND ECONOMY.

What does that mean in practical terms?

- The Federal Government should eliminate its annual deficit. Its budget must be balanced—this year, next year, and every year without exception.

- Government should no longer ask the Federal Reserve to monetize its debt.

- Government should stop borrowing money and begin repaying its massive loans.

- Government should refuse to engage in corporate welfare. It should not subsidize inefficient businesses or perpetuate their existence.

- Government should not be allowed to serve one group of citizens at the expense of another or at the expense of the nation as a whole. In keeping with this principle, upon which our nation was founded, all government aid to special interest groups should be eliminated—but only over a period of several years to give people time to adapt to the change.

- As government spending falls, taxes should be reduced, allowing individuals to channel their assets into savings and investment.

- The amount of paper money in circulation should be stabilized at present levels. It should not be increased or decreased since we want to avoid both runaway inflation and a deflationary collapse.

- We should return to a 100% gold-backed currency—but only after the budget has been balanced and the money supply stabilized at its current level.

If we take these steps, we can soon enter a time of unprecedented prosperity for America.[8] Some adjustments will be necessary. For one, we must learn to take greater responsibility for ourselves.

If we want to strengthen the economy, we must learn to see beyond our own immediate interests. We must cut our ties to old and inefficient ways of doing business and surrender all privileges which come at the expense of others. This could mean a gradual stream of bankruptcies as inefficient and archaic businesses are eliminated.

It will also mean a shift towards more useful employment, greater productivity, and the creation of more wealth for all of us.

NOTES

1. Second Chronicles 7:14. And if My people who are called by My name humble themselves and pray, and seek My face and turn from their wicked ways, then I will hear from heaven, will forgive their sin, and will heal their land.

2. Exodus 20:16. You shall not bear false witness against your neighbor.

3. Deuteronomy 16:19. You shall not distort justice; you shall not be partial, and you shall not take a bribe, for a bribe blinds the eyes of the wise and perverts the words of the righteous.

4. Proverbs 12:14. The deeds of a man's hands will return to him.

5. Deuteronomy 28:45. So all these curses shall come on you and pursue you and overtake you until you are destroyed, because you would not obey the Lord your God by keeping His commandments and His statutes which He commanded you.

6. John Bartlett, *Familiar Quotations* (Boston: Little, Brown and Company, 1980), p. 397.

7. Ibid., p. 374.

8. Proverbs 13:21. Adversity pursues sinners, but the righteous will be rewarded with prosperity.

PART TWO

8

PROTECTING YOURSELF
IN THE YEARS TO COME

Now that I see what is happening with the economy, it's frightening. What can I do to protect myself?

To protect yourself financially, you must understand the financial climate of the 1980's. It is essential that you know what investments to make. Many investments that were profitable in the past may become passports to financial disaster in these changing times.

IF YOU DO NOT RECOGNIZE THIS, YOU COULD BE HURT BADLY IN THE YEARS AHEAD.

Safety, not speculation, is the principle that will guide the 1980's as we enter a period of tremendous economic change.[1]

During this transition period, before we enter the prosperous times that lie ahead, you may be considered a genius if you simply hold on to what you have.

Some people could lose everything they own.

I don't want that to happen to me.

If you prepare for the future, it won't.

If you take steps to protect yourself and your family now, you will be comfortable during whatever storms may break in the future. Unfortunately, having enough money will not solve all of your problems.

Why not?

In recent years many books have been written about "how to cope with the coming bad times." Most authors prescribe gold, guns, survival food, and a house in the hills as a way of escaping the inevitable disaster. If these hard times do occur, their prescriptions may insure survival, but they will not insure sanity.

During a time of rapid change, mental preparation is essential. You must anticipate change and adapt as it comes your way. You must also be prepared to rely on yourself to get through whatever lies ahead.

Why?

If there is a severe crisis, or even if things get much worse, you may be on your own. The government will be limited in how much it can help you or anyone else. It will be up to you to preserve your sanity in the midst of tremendous change.

The only thing that will get you through times like these is self-sufficiency and the right attitude.

I think I'd feel better if I had more money and knew I couldn't lose it.

There are ways you can make more money and ways to protect yourself against financial loss. To do this, however, *you must understand what is happening in our economy today.* Many conventional investments will be destroyed in the years ahead if our economy gets much worse.

Which investments are you talking about?

Pension plans, bonds, insurance policies, and cash in checking or savings accounts. If inflation continues, returns on all of these investments will lag behind the increase in consumer prices, gradually decreasing the value of your assets.

If inflation gets out of control and makes the value of our currency worthless, people who have all their money tied up in this type of investment will be completely wiped out.

What if there is a depression instead?

If that happened, housing prices would fall, and so would the price of stocks. There would be many bankruptcies, and people who owned corporate or municipal bonds might be told there was a moratorium on the repayment of all debt. Many corporations and cities could default altogether.

Insurance companies would also be hard-pressed to refund their investors' money. Banks and savings and loans could fold. If all your money is tied up in these investments, you could lose everything—overnight.

The investment climate in America has changed over the past twenty years. You can no longer guarantee your financial security by making conventional investments alone. *Yet, there are steps you can take to protect yourself.*

ONCE YOU LEARN THE RULES WHICH GOVERN INVESTMENT IN A TURBULENT ECONOMY, YOU CAN PLACE YOUR SAVINGS WHERE THEY WILL WORK FOR YOU, SAFE FROM THE RAVAGES OF INFLATION OR DEPRESSION.

My brother-in-law has been talking about the economy for years. He says inflation eats up your savings and that it is foolish to save money when prices are constantly rising. He says it's much smarter to borrow money now and repay your debts later with dollars that are worth much less. Is he right? Is there any point in saving money at all?

Yes, there definitely is, despite what your brother-in-law says. Inflation destroys conventional investments, but that does not mean there are no profitable and secure ways to save money in today's economy. There are. You just need to learn about them.

At the moment our economy is fragile, yet stable in the sense that if you have personal problems, there is always somewhere you can turn for help. Unemployment compensation, food stamps, and a host of other federal programs are available to people with financial difficulties. There are also many jobs available, even though 'unemployment' is high.

If we were to experience a major crisis, however, this situation could change overnight. You could lose your job, and there might not be another job immediately available. And if the hardship were widespread, you might find that the only person you could turn to for help would be

YOURSELF.

That is why you want to become self-sufficient now. You want to ensure that you can weather whatever storms lie ahead without depending on anyone else for support. To do that you must have money set aside.

What if you're in debt? It's hard enough to save money when you're being hit by taxes and inflation. How can you possibly get ahead if you're in debt?

The secret is to save part of your income each month and to use it in two ways:

   1. to repay your debt, and

   2. to save some money for yourself.

By doing that you will gradually work your way out of debt while enjoying the satisfaction of watching your savings grow.

THE TIME FOR SAVING IS NOW.[2]

We are not necessarily talking about a large amount of money. Even $2,000—properly managed—could spare you a lot of grief in the months and years ahead.

What if a person doesn't have any money? What about my brother-in-law, for example?

As we said, *the time for saving is now.* If people would form the habit of saving ten or fifteen percent of their income, they would soon accumulate enough to see them through any future problems. Another benefit of saving will be

PEACE OF MIND.

If we are able to solve our problems without a crisis, fine. This is exactly what we are hoping for. People who have money set aside will be in a position to enjoy life even more once the danger is past.

Should we experience real hardship, however, before better times arrive, having your money safely invested will be a stroke of genius. Your "insurance policy" will have paid off by keeping you financially secure, regardless of what goes on around you.

Alright, let's say I have $10,000. What should I do with my money?

The first thing we should tell you is this:

DON'T PUT ALL YOUR EGGS IN ONE BASKET.

At this time, we do not know whether the inflationary cycle of the past forty years will continue, whether a depression will set in, or if there will be a soft landing.

What is a soft landing?

A soft landing is a gradual decline in the rate of inflation, a steady growth of business and employment, and the re-emergence of a sound economy. Obviously that would be the best path, but we don't know how things will turn out yet. Therefore, you should be prepared for almost anything.

BECAUSE NO ONE KNOWS WHAT IS GOING TO HAPPEN WITH THE ECONOMY, THERE IS NO SINGLE INVESTMENT WE CAN ADVISE YOU TO MAKE AND GUARANTEE THAT IT WILL PROTECT YOUR SAVINGS IN THE YEARS TO COME.

If we knew that inflation would continue, we would tell you to put all your money in precious metals and in currencies like the Swiss franc, which are not as affected by inflation as the American dollar. However, we do not know that continued inflation is inevitable. We could have a depression instead, in which case the value of these "hard" assets might actually decline in relation to the dollar. As the supply of paper money became increasingly tight, its value would rise, making dollars the best thing to own.

What if there is a soft landing?

If that happens, businesses will boom, the stock market will rise dramatically, and we will all enjoy a higher standard of living. The most profitable investment you could make under those circumstances would be in a productive enterprise, although cash savings would also be safe with the threat of inflation gone.

Of course, not all stocks will prove equally successful. Some established businesses may fail to adapt to the needs of the future, while many new businesses will emerge to meet the public's demand for goods and services that have not been previously available.

What exactly are you talking about?

To give an example of how this process is already underway, we'll repeat a story some friends from San Diego recently told us. A few years ago some people there opened a large grocery store carrying high quality, natural foods. They did a tremendous business and drew many customers away from the older chain stores in San Diego. Some outlets of these older stores soon closed, while this new grocery store expanded to several more locations.

The eating habits of many Americans are changing. We are becoming more aware of the quality and the nutritional value of the food we buy. We are also becoming more selective and demanding.

Businesses which anticipate these needs and meet them will prosper in the years ahead; those which do not will gradually fold.

The tea business is another good example of how this process works. Years ago, few Americans had ever heard of herbal tea. By now, however, most of us know about the negative side effects of caffeine. As a result, many of us drink decaffeinated coffee and herbal tea instead.

The people who founded Celestial Seasonings, the largest manufacturer of herbal tea in America, anticipated this change years ago. Their business has grown tremendously, to the point where the giants of the industry, including Lipton, have acknowledged their success by entering the market for herbal tea. This is a market with a huge growth potential as the dietary habits of Americans continue to change.

What exactly are you suggesting? Should I buy stock in a tea company? Should I buy gold? Silver? Real estate?

Because we do not know what the future holds, you must diversify your assets. What we suggest is this:

- The ultimate protection against inflation is gold. You should own some gold because it maintains its purchasing power in the face of rising inflation. Gold will see you through a crisis if our currency becomes worthless.

- You should keep some cash in a high-yield money market fund which invests in short-term Treasury securities. In this way, you can protect yourself from inflation and depression at the same time. The interest you earn will protect you from inflation, while the cash savings will pull you through a depression or tight credit squeeze. Ironically, Treasury Bills are probably the safest cash investment available at this time.

- If you have enough money, it would be a good idea to own your own home.

- If you have extra money to invest, you may also want to buy stock. However, judging the potential for success of any specific company is a complex and difficult task—one best left to a qualified professional.

ABOVE ALL ELSE, DON'T GAMBLE WITH YOUR MONEY. THAT IS THE SUREST WAY TO LOSE IT.[3]

During a time of financial instability, you may be tempted to speculate in real estate, precious metals, or other commodities. However, this is a dangerous thing to do.

When a person gambles, they have a chance to make lots of money, but *they can also lose everything they own.*[4]

The investment advice we are offering is not for gamblers. It is for people who want a sure thing.

NOTES

1. Proverbs 14:16.   A wise man is cautious and turns away from e.
but a fool is arrogant and careless.

2. First Corinthians 16:2.   On the first day of every week let each one
of you put aside and save, as he may prosper.

3. Proverbs 14:15–16.   The naive believe everything but the prudent
man considers his steps.

A wise man is cautious and turns away from evil, but a fool is
arrogant and careless.

4. Proverbs 28:20.   He who makes haste to be rich will not go
unpunished.

9

GOLD

Let's get specific now. What should I do with my money?

As we have said before, be sure to cover all your bases. Among other things, that means

INVEST IN HARD MONEY.

What do you mean by hard money?

We mean gold, because its intrinsic value is recognized throughout the world.

Is gold real money?

Money is whatever people accept as payment for goods and services. For thousands of years, gold has been viewed as the *ultimate* money. It does not tarnish, rust or deteriorate. It is virtually indestructible. Even more important,

GOLD CANNOT BE MANIPULATED BY GOVERNMENTS, THE WAY PAPER MONEY CAN.

Historically, paper money has been nothing but a receipt for gold in a vault. Any person could take their paper notes to a bank, ask for gold, and receive it. When that was true, a "gold standard" was in effect, and everyone knew that the supply of paper money was limited. Its value was stable because it was tied to the supply of gold. No one could change or manipulate that.[1]

Most governments, of course, have never liked this situation.

Why not?

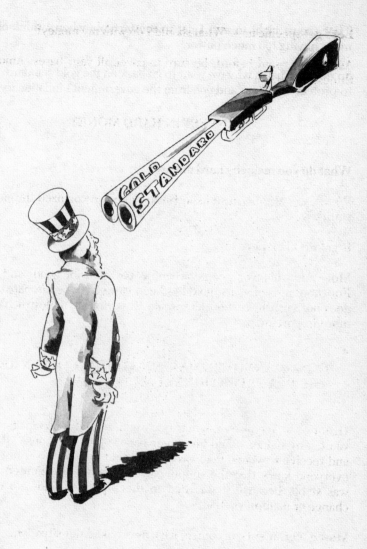

The gold standard prevents a government from controlling its nation's money supply. It places economic power in the hands of each individual, rather than allowing that power to be concentrated in the hands of government.

That seems right to me. I get uncomfortable when I think of government having too much power.

So do we. That is why we want to go back on the gold standard. We want to protect ourselves and *you* from the government's inflationary policies.

Under a full gold standard, the government is not free to inflate its nation's currency. It is not free to confiscate, secretly and unobserved, the wealth of its citizens through the hidden tax of inflation.

Today we no longer have a gold standard in America. We have allowed government to seize control of our economic lives.

What can we do to change this situation?

We can try to reverse government policy. We can demand that the law be used for no purpose other than what was intended by the United States Constitution—to protect the life, liberty, and property of every American.

Whenever the law benefits one person at the expense of another, by doing what an individual himself cannot do without committing a crime, the law has been perverted and should be changed. Of course, the people who profit from these laws may resist.[2] Many people have been taught to expect government subsidies as their birthright. For this reason, even as you act to change the direction of our government, you should take care to protect yourself from government policies now in force. These policies are unlikely to change overnight.

What can I do to protect myself?

For one thing, you can buy gold. By owning gold, you shield yourself from the irresponsible economic policies of our government. You become immune to the silent tax of inflation. Gold will maintain its purchasing power as the value of the paper dollar continues to erode.

People who understand the nature of money usually prefer gold to unbacked paper currency. They do not want to base their financial security on a government's promise to pay its debts, *especially when they know that such promises have been broken by governments many times in the past.*

What are you talking about?

We are talking about all of the runaway inflations of the past—in Germany, in China, in France, and even in the United States. During the Revolutionary War, our Continental currency became worthless.

But isn't gold unnecessary today? I've heard people say that it's just a barbaric relic, without any monetary value in a civilized country.

They're right, in a sense. Gold *is* a barbaric relic. Unfortunately, man is still so primitive that he must use this yellow metal to regulate himself —to limit how much paper money he creates.

GOLD STANDS FOR DISCIPLINE. A gold-backed currency means that you cannot have everything you want when you want it, *unless you have worked to earn it.* Under a gold standard, no one can create paper money unless they have enough gold to serve as backing. The government is thus regulated by law. It cannot create money out of thin air to finance its programs. It must ask the people for permission to spend *by asking them to pay taxes.*

I still have my doubts. I've heard people say that gold is just a speculative commodity, essentially useless unless you happen to like fine jewelry.

We've heard that story too. But think a minute and ask yourself:

If gold is a useless commodity, why did the government fill a large building to the ceiling with gold bars and then assign the army to protect it? Why does Fort Knox exist?

If a person told me he was against drinking, but I saw that his garage was full of whiskey, I would wonder whether he was telling the truth.

Now if that still does not convince you to buy gold, consider this: the richest banks and governments in the world keep only one thing other than paper money in their vaults.

What is that?

GOLD.

GOLD IS REAL MONEY. If paper currencies become worthless, international payments will have to be made in gold. Due to accelerating inflation, gold may be the *only* form of money that retains its value throughout the 1980's.[3] Large banks know that. So do governments. That is why they are planning ahead, filling their vaults with gold.

SHOULDN'T YOU?

But isn't gold a dangerous investment? I've seen its price go up or down as much as $100 in one day. How do I know that the price won't collapse as soon as I've put my money in gold?

To feel comfortable buying gold, you have to understand the nature of this investment. You must realize that the price of gold fluctuates from day to day because it is a barometer of the world's turmoil and fear. Whenever there is bad news, people buy gold; and whenever things seem to get better, its price tends to go down. This makes gold a dangerous investment for anyone who would buy it one day and sell it the next. We are not advising you to do that, however. *We do not want you to speculate in gold. We want you to buy some gold and hold on to it as a form of insurance.* Then, daily fluctuations in its price will not affect you.

**IT IS ESSENTIAL
TO UNDERSTAND THAT
GOLD IS A LONG-TERM INVESTMENT.**

Gold is a form of insurance. You don't cancel your insurance policy because you suddenly think you will not have an accident. By having enough insurance, you enjoy peace of mind.

But you must think that gold is headed up in the long run.

That's right. If you talk about what will happen to gold tomorrow or next week, it is pure speculation. It would be like putting some food on the sidewalk and betting whether a dog would come by in the next ten minutes and eat it. Who knows? It is just a matter of chance.

On the other hand, if you were asked whether an animal would eat the food within the next month, your answer would most likely be yes. At that point, you are no longer talking about gambling. You are talking about something quite likely to occur.

The same thing is true with gold. Most people do not understand gold. They do not understand that its price is directly related to the value of the paper dollar. They do not know, for example, that to have a 100% gold-backed currency in the United States, *the price of gold would have to be over $1,850 an ounce*.

Instead of knowing the facts and understanding why the price of gold is likely to rise in the months and years ahead, most people look at the day to day price fluctuations of gold and decide that it is too dangerous for them. Unfortunately, if there ever comes a time when our paper money is worthless and everyone is demanding gold, it will be too late for them to change their minds. Their savings will already have been lost.

But are you *sure* the price of gold will stay high or keep rising indefinitely?

The price of gold will continue to rise as long as the value of paper money goes down. As long as there is fear and uncertainty in the world, the price of gold will remain high. People cling to gold during times of rapid change because it offers them certainty and security—qualities which are noticeably lacking in the outside world.

Yet when our current crisis is over, there is no better candidate to serve as international money than gold, which has served this function for thousands of years.

You see, despite all appearances to the contrary, the value of gold is stable. It is a lack of confidence in paper money that causes the price of gold to fluctuate wildly. Gold has not increased in value over the past fifty years. *It is the value of paper money which has gone down.*

Today, a $20 gold coin will buy the same amount of goods it did fifty years ago. Obviously, you cannot say the same of a $20 bill.

In 1930, you could walk into any clothing store in the country, buy the best suit in stock, and pay for your purchase with a one-ounce gold coin. Today, one ounce of gold will still buy you the finest suit in town. A $20 bill, on the other hand, may not even pay for a shirt to wear with it.

What we are saying is: *gold maintains its purchasing power through the years.*

When you hold only paper dollars instead of gold, you leave yourself vulnerable to external factors and events. The government can print unlimited quantities of paper money, making what you own worthless. Under our present banking system, the same thing can occur through a large expansion of credit.

For the past fifty years, our supply of paper money has increased dramatically, decreasing its value many times over. The process through which this occurs is so subtle that few people realize what is happening. Even though we are faced with inflation day by day, most of us do not know how to protect ourselves.

Money is like fuel. It gives you the power to do things. You need that fuel in order to function in life.

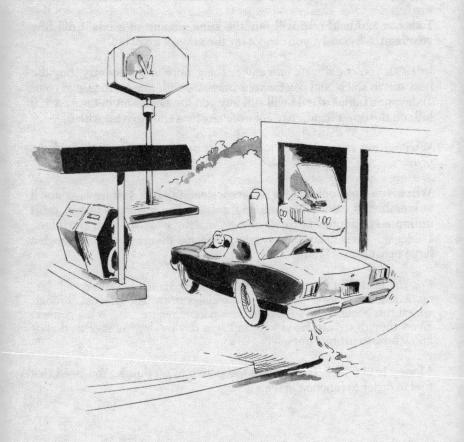

If you suddenly saw that your car had a hole in its gas tank, you would stop at the first service station you could find to fix it. Because you could actually see the gasoline leaking out onto the road, your reaction would be to do something immediately. You would never let it go on and on.

Yet when it comes to money and the purchasing power of our dollar, we let its value decline day by day. We let the situation go on because the cause of inflation, and its effects, are less visible. We feel frustrated and angry, but our education has not prepared us to deal with this kind of emergency. We blame others for the leak and try to pump more fuel into our tanks. The leak remains, however, because we are not doing anything to fix it.

> BY OWNING GOLD, YOU CAN FIX THAT LEAK.
> BY RETURNING TO A FULL GOLD STANDARD,
> WE CAN STOP THE GOVERNMENT FROM IN-
> FLATING OUR MONEY SUPPLY.

We must stop inflation at its source. We must prevent the banks and government from increasing our money supply. But in the meantime, if you own gold, you can prevent inflation from gradually draining you of your assets.

How much should I invest in gold?

That depends on how comfortable you feel with it. A lot of people make the mistake of trying to figure this out intellectually. What really matters is what makes *you* feel comfortable.

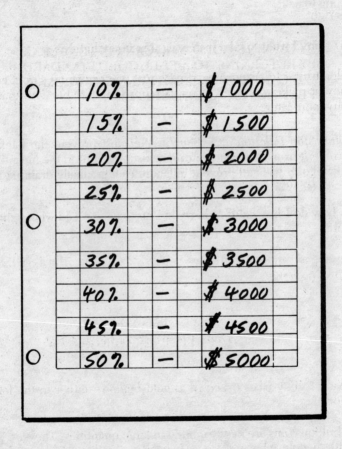

10%	—	$1000
15%	—	$1500
20%	—	$2000
25%	—	$2500
30%	—	$3000
35%	—	$3500
40%	—	$4000
45%	—	$4500
50%	—	$5000

It might be useful to write on paper the numbers 10%, 20% . . . all the way up to 50%, and then assign a dollar value to each of these percentages. For example, you said you have $10,000 to invest. Beside 10% write $1,000; beside 15% write $1,500, and so forth. Then look at each figure and find out what you are comfortable with.

I'll do that, but what percentage do you recommend?

We suggest that you have at least 15% of your net worth invested in gold—preferably more.

Up to 50%?

That's right.

I don't think I want to take such a big step immediately.

You don't have to. You can start with just one or two ounces of gold to see how it makes you feel. Then if you are comfortable with that, you can buy more later.

Should I buy it right away or should I wait?

That would be like waiting to get insurance on your house until after a break-in. By then it would be too late.

Well, how do I buy gold? Where do I go to get it? And where should I keep it?

There are any number of ways you can buy gold. The first thing to remember, though, is:

YOU WANT GOLD CONTENT,

NOT PRETTY PACKAGING.

You want to buy what is known as gold *bullion*—either in the form of coins or bars.

Gold bullion coins are newly minted in large quantities. They are popular with people who wish to own gold in small, portable, and easily stored units. We recommend this for at least the first $10,000 of your investment in gold.

It costs a certain amount of money to mint, ship, and sell these coins. Therefore, when you buy a gold bullion coin, you will have to pay what is known as a premium to cover this cost. The premium generally runs 3-5% of the price of gold itself. In most states there is no sales tax on gold bullion, provided you invest $1,000 or more.

The most popular bullion coins sold today are the 1-ounce Canadian Maple Leaf, the 1-ounce Krugerrand from South Africa, the Austrian 100 Corona, and the Mexican 50 Peso. A new, 1-ounce coin from Mexico which recently appeared on the market should also prove very popular, along with one-half, one-quarter, and one-tenth ounce gold coins. All of these coins can probably be bought from a coin dealer near your home. Before buying, however, it is best to shop around since premiums can vary from store to store.

We suggest you contact a number of dealers to compare prices. You should call after 3:00 p.m., Eastern Standard Time, when the commodity exchange markets have already closed, fixing the price of gold for the day.

Isn't gold too expensive for most people to afford?

For people with smaller incomes, gold can be purchased in one-tenth or one-quarter ounce coins. This makes gold easily affordable for almost everyone.

What about rare coins? Should I buy any of those?

No.

The value of old coins—such as the British Sovereign, the U.S. $20 gold piece, or the French Napoleon—largely depends upon their rarity. The price you must pay for one of these coins is always much higher than the market price of gold.

The same is true if you buy little wafers of gold to wear around your neck, or miniature reproductions of gold coins. Only 10% to 30% of what you pay is for gold. The rest is for pretty packaging, advertising, and other expenses.

If there is no store in your area which sells bullion coins, there are a number of major dealers who ship nationwide, and can provide you with what you need:

DEAK-PERARA
1800 K Street N.W.
Washington, D.C. 20006
(800) 424-1186
(202) 872-1233

INVESTMENT RARITIES
One Appletree Square
Minneapolis, Minnesota 55420
(800) 328-1860
(612) 853-0700

Do I want the coins delivered to my home? Wouldn't it be better for the dealer to keep them in storage until I need them?

No, definitely not. If you let the dealer keep your coins until an emergency comes, you might not be able to get them.

YOU SHOULD TAKE PHYSICAL POSSESSION OF ANY GOLD COINS YOU BUY. Never leave your gold in the possession of a dealer. He could go bankrupt tomorrow. Then, where would you be?

Where should I keep my gold?

It should be someplace you feel is safe. Maybe you would feel comfortable keeping a few coins in your home where you will have immediate access to them if you need them. You can keep the rest in a safe deposit box at a bank, or even better, with a private company that rents safe deposit boxes to the general public.

When you buy coins, you should also pay for them in cash. You want your ownership to be known only to you and to your immediate family. That way you minimize the danger of theft. You also protect yourself against government seizure should the ownership of gold be outlawed.

Outlawed? How could it be against the law to own gold?

All Congress has to do is pass a law making it illegal to own gold. Many people in our government hate gold because it limits their ability to expand the money supply. If their backs were ever pressed against the wall, they could become desperate and ban private ownership of gold.

Outlawing gold is unconstitutional. It is also morally wrong. But with the police enforcing the law, you would still have to deal with it.

But if it is unconstitutional, how could such a law be passed?

Legislators who approved it would have to be ignorant of the Constitution; or else, in the name of a "national emergency," violate the Constitution by assuming powers not granted to them. This happened in 1934 when it became illegal for Americans to own gold bullion.

What! You mean it was illegal to own gold at one time?

Yes, it was illegal to own gold for over forty years. In 1934, Americans were forced to exchange their gold and gold certificates for bank notes issued by the Federal Reserve.

The only problem was that Congress exceeded the authority granted to it by the United States Constitution. The federal government has never been given the power to ban private ownership of gold or to declare paper money to be "legal tender for all debts, public and private." It does have the authority to "coin money" and standardize its value (Article I, Section 8, paragraph 5 of the United States Constitution), but it does *not* have the authority to tell people what kind of money they must accept in exchange for good and services.[4]

Likewise, the various states were prohibited from issuing an unbacked paper currency under Article I, Section 10 of the Constitution, which reads: "No state shall make any thing but gold and silver coin a tender in payment of debts."

OUR FOUNDING FATHERS DENIED GOVERNMENT THE POWER TO TRANSFORM PAPER INTO "GOLD" BECAUSE THEY UNDERSTOOD INFLATION.[5] They knew that if the government could print thousands of pieces of paper, declare them to be money, and force people to accept that money in exchange for their goods and services, it would acquire tremendous power over the life of every American. Your right to keep the product of your work would be undermined by the government through the hidden tax of inflation.

Then why did the government pass that law in 1934, making it illegal to own gold?

Special interests which benefit from inflation made sure that it was passed.

Which special interests?

Large banking interests, for the most part. Banks profit greatly from inflation. When they are allowed to create money out of thin air, lend it to you, and receive interest on the money you have borrowed, it is clear that something strange is going on. The bank makes money. You get your loan. But somewhere along the line, someone else is losing since inflation makes their money worth less.

When America was on the gold standard, the value of the dollar was strictly tied to gold. Any time you had a paper dollar, you could go to a bank or to the Treasury Department and exchange it for a specific amount of gold. During and after World War I, however, the amount of paper money in circulation was increased dramatically by the Federal Reserve. By the time Franklin D. Roosevelt came to office in 1933, America was facing a crisis. The banks and government did not have enough gold to redeem all their paper dollars at the old, standard price.

Instead of honoring its commitment to exchange a fixed weight of gold for every dollar in circulation, our government did just the opposite. It banned private ownership of gold and declared Federal Reserve Notes, issued by banks, to be legal tender—the official money of the United States of America. As a result, inflation has been allowed to continue, and there is almost no limit to how many paper dollars the banks and government can create.

No limit at all?

The main factor now limiting inflation is public mistrust of the dollar. People are wary of inflation. When it seems to be getting out of hand, they turn to gold, silver, foreign currencies—anything to escape the falling dollar.

People who benefit from inflation dislike gold. It represents an alternative to paper money, an escape route, a storehouse of value which is immune to inflation. In order to protect their monopoly—their control of our money supply—powerful banking interests could once again seek to ban private ownership of gold in America.

Not without a fight from me!

How would you stop them?

I'd write my Congressman and my Senators. I'd tell them they would never get re-elected if they voted for something like that.

If they thought it would cost them their job, most Congressmen *would* refuse to confiscate your gold. Still, you want to be prepared for whatever happens. That's why you should keep whatever gold coins you buy in your own possession, rather than in someone else's hands.

Several large investment firms now offer what are known as gold accumulation programs. You send them a check, and they buy a certain amount of gold for you, which they store in a bank in New York. Obviously, this leaves you vulnerable to government confiscation—you and all the other clients who have stored their gold in that vault.

The purpose of owning gold is to make yourself independent of others in every possible way. You want to diversify your holdings in order to minimize risk. For this reason, we also suggest that if you buy more than twenty thousand dollars worth of gold, you keep some of it overseas, in Switzerland.

Why Switzerland? I'm not a movie star or a criminal! What do I need with a Swiss bank account?

It will give you an added degree of protection if you have a lot of money to invest.

The Swiss have a long tradition of respecting other people's lives and property. That is why they have been politically neutral for so many centuries. It is also why so many people from all parts of the world have entrusted them with their money. The Swiss are not about to confiscate your gold or impose heavy taxes on you.

Do you want me to send all my money to Switzerland?

By no means. Just a portion of your assets, if that. If you don't have much money, don't worry. Just keep whatever gold you buy at home or in a safe deposit box. If you have a lot of money, though, we suggest you look into the possibility of a Swiss bank account. It could be worth the trouble in the long run.

What about foreign currencies?

When the dollar declines in value, strong currencies, such as the Swiss franc, usually go up. By keeping a portion of your assets in Swiss francs, you can protect yourself from a decline in the value of the dollar.

Then these currencies serve the same function as gold.

Gold is your first line of defense against inflation. But if you are very wealthy, other assets, such as the Swiss franc, can serve as a valuable second line of defense.

Why do you recommend Swiss francs instead of some other currency?

Inflation is lower in Switzerland than anywhere else in the world, and the Swiss franc is 40% backed by gold.

Are the banks in Switzerland any safer than ours in America?

Much safer. Swiss bankers, in general, are known for their integrity. Their banks are usually run in a sound, conservative way.[6]

During the Great Depression, when 10,000 banks in America failed, as did thousands of others throughout the world . . .

only one bank in Switzerland was forced to close its doors. Even there, no one lost money. The Swiss government saw that all depositors were repaid in full.

How can I open an account at a Swiss bank?

First, you must decide what services you want to receive from a bank. For example, you would probably want to open a gold account, through which you purchase gold and have a bank store it for you. The gold you buy would be yours alone. It would not be listed on the bank's balance sheet. Should anything go wrong with the bank, it could not use your gold to pay its debts.

You might also want a savings account denominated in Swiss francs, or a managed account. Whatever you decide, you must select a bank which can best meet your needs. Then, you can open an account with that bank; forward your money via cashier's check, money order, or wire transfer; and instruct your bank what to do with the money when it arrives.

This sounds complicated.

It is somewhat complicated. But if you are interested in the subject, we recommend that you read a book which will give you all the details, for example:

> *Harry Browne's Complete Guide to Swiss Banks.*
> (Harry Browne, McGraw-Hill, 1976.) $14.95

> or

> *The Swiss Banking Handbook: A Complete*
> *Manual for Practical Investors.* (Robert
> Roethenmund, Books in Focus, 1980.) $8.95.

Once my money is in Switzerland, how can I get it out? If I never go there, how will I have access to it?

You can write or call your bank and ask them to sell any or all of the gold you have stored there. They will sell it immediately, and you will be paid the current price of gold on the Zurich exchange. Then, the money will be forwarded to you immediately. If you are in a rush for the money, your Swiss bank can wire it to an American account. If not, they will mail you a check.

At one point you said there were other kinds of hard money I could buy to give myself greater diversity and protection. What were you talking about?

A strong currency, such as the Swiss franc, is one such hedge. Another is silver. If inflation ever gets completely out of control, the dollar will become worthless, and a new currency will have to be established. During the interim period, silver coins such as those made in the United States before 1965 might come to serve as a means of exchange. They would be much more practical for making day-to-day purchases than gold coins such as the Maple Leaf or the Krugerrand. After all, you don't pay for a bag of spinach with a hundred dollar bill.

"Is this a joke or are you crazy? You're giving me a $2,000 coin to pay for a loaf of bread!"

Holding these coins is a kind of insurance against the worst that could happen. We advise that you do this only as a precautionary measure, however, rather than as a major investment.

What about buying large quantities of silver? Wouldn't that give me the same protection as gold?

Gold and silver have both been used as money for thousands of years. Both are durable, scarce, and divorced from anyone's promise to pay. For this reason, silver is often classified along with gold as a major monetary metal.

Today, however, silver is used almost exclusively for industrial purposes. Its value is closely tied to industrial demand. Should either hyperinflation or a major depression occur, industry and commerce would be disrupted. Then a glut of silver could appear on the market as supply outstripped demand.

Because of its vulnerability, we advise you to hold only a minor, secondary position in silver—at most, 5% of your net worth. Its primary purpose, in a time of emergency, would be to provide for your day to day shopping needs. Beyond that, you are betting on a commodity, rather than investing in a monetary good.

Some people claim that silver has a greater appreciation potential than gold. Are they right?

At the present time, perhaps it does. Current industrial demand for silver far exceeds new supplies. But that does not mean you should buy huge quantities of silver. Owning some silver is fine, but your primary protection should be in gold.

No one knows what the future holds. That is why you want to buy gold. It is your best insurance policy against inflation.

NOTES

1. Proverbs 16:11.   A just balance and scales belong to the Lord; all the weights of the bag are His concern.

2. Frederic Bastiat, *The Law*, translated from the French by Dean Russell (Irvington-on-Hudson, New York: Foundation for Economic Education, 1950), p. 21.

3. Proverbs 11:1.   A false balance is an abomination to the Lord, but a just weight is His delight.

4. As Daniel Webster wrote, "If we understand, by currency, the legal money of the country, and that which constitutes a lawful tender for debts, and is the statute measure of value, then undoubtedly, nothing is included but gold and silver. Most unquestionably, *there is no legal tender, and there can be no legal tender in this country under the authority of this government or any other, but gold and silver,* either the coinage of our mints or foreign coins at rates regulated by Congress. *This is a constitutional principle, perfectly plain and of the very highest importance.* The states are expressly prohibited from making anything but gold and silver a tender in payment of debts, and although no such expressed prohibition is applied to Congress, yet as Congress has no power granted to it in this respect but to coin money and to regulate the value of foreign coins, *it clearly has no power to substitute paper or anything else for coin* as a tender in payment of debts in a discharge of contracts...."

(Emphasis added.) From Representative Ron Paul and Lewis Lehrman, *The Case For Gold* (Washington, D.C.: Cato Institute, 1982), p. 169.

5. "[Gold] is the most perfect medium because it will preserve its own level; because, having intrinsic and universal value, it can never die in our hands.... [Paper money] is liable to be abused, has been, is, and forever will be abused, in every country in which it is permitted."—Thomas Jefferson.

6. Nevertheless, we recommend that you choose a bank carefully, dealing only with those which are highly liquid (that is, which have

a high ratio of convertible assets to money on deposit). Several banks which, through the years, have met this criterion are:

> Bank Indiana (Suisse) S.A.
> 50 Avenue de la Gare
> CH-1001 Lausanne, Switzerland
>
> Foreign Commerce Bank
> Belariastrasse 82
> CH-8038 Zurich, Switzerland
>
> Cambio + Valorenbank
> Utoquai 55
> CH-8008 Zurich, Switzerland
>
> Bankinstitut Zurich
> Grossmuensterplatz 9
> CH-8021 Zurich, Switzerland.

Although the authors of this book mention, as a service to their readers, the names of several widely respected precious metals dealers, no-load mutual funds, and Swiss banks, this does not constitute an endorsement of these firms. The authors have no connection—directly or indirectly—with any of these firms, and thus cannot guarantee their continued performance or reliability.

10

ANTIQUES, GEMS,
AND REAL ESTATE

Aren't there other things I should buy to protect myself against inflation?

What do you have in mind?

Antiques. Real estate. Collectibles. A lot of things besides gold and silver have risen in price over the past ten years.

That's true. During the 1970's people began to expect that their money would be worth less the longer they held onto it. As a result, they started looking for places to invest their money. Some people were willing to buy almost anything—stamps, baseball cards, old wooden barrels, even comic books.

Why would anyone want to buy an old wooden barrel?

Some people assume that anything old and rare must be more valuable than something made in a factory today. This is why antiques and other collectibles have become such popular inflation hedges.

Not long ago, a small town in Kansas replaced all of its parking meters. The old ones were taken to city hall, and a sale was announced. People came from miles around to buy them.

What makes something valuable is not its supply alone, but its supply in relation to demand.

If you buy an antique because you like it, that's fine. You will enjoy having it in your home, and if you are lucky, it may even rise in value over the years. But if you are buying art or antiques as inflation hedges alone, there are several things you ought to know.

The value of most collectibles has risen greatly over the past ten years because there has been a flight from the dollar into anything old and rare. Some people who bought early, when prices were low, have been able to make money investing in collectibles. But the question now arises, as we enter a period of tremendous economic change, whether the price of these objects is overinflated.

If you are thinking about buying collectibles now—or keeping what you already have as a form of economic security—ask yourself the following questions:

"If there is a crisis, if I lose my job and have to sell these things to get food for my family, how valuable will they be at that time? And how quickly will I be able to sell them?"

Certainly, a parking meter will not be of much value to anyone during hard times. For a person to give you something they value, such as food, you will have to offer them something they value just as highly in return. During a time of economic chaos, few things qualify.

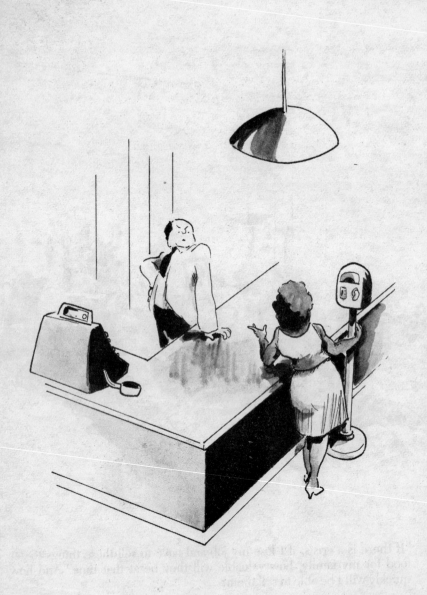

"I want you to buy this antique parking meter. In fact, I'll give it to you for $700."

"What do you mean, you won't buy it? This bronzed monkey tail is worth at least $12,000!"

"This is a rare painting. I tell you it's priceless!"

"All I'm asking is $10,000 for this ancient Chinese coin. I've been told it's worth two or three times that much."

Trying to sell any of these items during turbulent economic times would be like being trapped in a burning house.

What do you mean?

These people are trapped with investments that are hard to sell. If they do eventually find someone who will buy these things, they will probably have to take a loss. Not only are they unable to sell their collectibles quickly, but they may also lose a large part of their investment. The whole question here is one of liquidity.

Being *liquid* means owning something people will buy whenever you want to sell.

LIQUIDITY PROVIDES YOU WITH PROTECTION AND SECURITY. YOU DON'T WANT TO BE TIED TO ILLIQUID INVESTMENTS WHICH SHOW A LARGE PROFIT ON PAPER BUT ARE DIFFICULT TO SELL IN A CRUNCH.

If you are tied to illiquid investments during an economic crisis, you may not be able to escape in safety.

What is a liquid investment?

A liquid investment is anything that can easily be sold if you have to. It is one step removed from the money you use to make your daily purchases. A liquid investment can be turned into cash or traded for whatever food, shelter, or clothing you may need.

IT IS YOUR BEST FINANCIAL PROTECTION
IN A TIME OF UPHEAVAL.

When you talk about liquid investments, do you mean something like gold?

That's right. Gold, silver, or U.S. Treasury Bills.

What about precious gems like diamonds, emeralds, or rubies?

Their price could rise in the future, but we do not recommend them.

Why not?

Precious stones are neither the safest nor the most liquid investment you can make. If you have to sell them, they are usually hard to get rid of at a fair price.

Does that apply to diamonds too?

Right now, the diamond market is tightly controlled by a syndicate which owns or controls nearly every diamond field in the world. The supply of investment grade diamonds on the world market has been limited for years to increase the price of those which are sold. As a result, any investment you make in diamonds can be jeopardized by events in some distant part of the world. What you want is financial security, rather than participating in a controlled market.

What about real estate as an investment? I know a lot of people who have made a killing in real estate.

362

Real estate has been a popular inflation hedge for the past twenty years. However, in deciding what to do with your money now, you must ask yourself, "What is the future of real estate? Are current high prices here to stay? And if I had to sell my property during a crisis, would I be able to do it without a loss?"

Are you saying the price of real estate could go down?

That already happened in most parts of the country during the 1981-82 recession. The price of housing in America has risen much faster than our population for the past thirty years. Whenever the price of something is inflated for a long time, people can't imagine prices ever coming back down. In order to understand why prices may decline further, however, we must understand how they got so high in the first place.

I've always wondered how that happened. The cost of housing is astronomical. I'm afraid my children won't be able to afford a house when they become adults.

At least four major factors were involved in the dramatic rise of real estate prices: the availability of credit, tax advantages to property owners, inflation, and the growing number of speculators in the real estate market.

Easy credit encouraged people to bid up the price of land by letting them pay more for property than they could otherwise afford. As you know, most people do not pay cash when they buy a house. For almost forty years Americans have been buying real estate with low downpayments and thirty-year loans subsidized by the federal government. The price you will pay if the money comes from your own pocket, and what you will pay if you are using someone else's money are two very different things.

Recognizing all the advantages of owning property, many people entered the real estate market hoping to make a quick profit. As long as people could afford the mortgage payments, they were willing to pay whatever they had to in order to buy a home. It was the old story of buy now and pay later. "I promise." Remember?

By now, however, the inflated cost of housing, combined with high interest rates, have put mortgage payments beyond the reach of most Americans.

In 1971, Americans had to spend an average of 19% of their income to make payments on an average home. By 1981, the cost of mortgage payments had risen to 32% of their monthly income.

As a result, the demand for real estate at such high prices began to fall. If high interest rates return, we can expect a further decline in the price of real estate in the next few years.

That still seems unlikely.

It seems unlikely unless you understand that current prices are artificially high and thus subject to correction. The 1960's and 1970's real estate boom was triggered by inflation and by everyone's assumption that inflation would continue to increase the value of their property. If inflation comes to an end or if we enter a deflationary period, prices may fall considerably.

Real estate is a highly illiquid investment. You may claim your home is worth $120,000; but you don't know if that's true until someone puts the money in your hand. If you own gold or foreign currency, you can pick up the newspaper each morning and see how much your assets are worth. You can sell your gold immediately. There will always be a buyer. When you own real estate, however, it may not be easy to find someone willing to buy. In a declining market, it could be next to impossible.

You don't want me to sell my home, do you?

Definitely not. We are discussing real estate as an investment, rather than as a consumer good. But if you are *heavily* invested in real estate, you might want to consider selling some of it now, rather than waiting for prices to fall as they may in the years to come.

During a time of transition, only two types of assets retain their full value: those which increase your enjoyment of life, if you can afford to own them, and those which are readily marketable to others.

During the economic collapse of Germany, following World Wars I and II, a lot of pianos, furniture, and art changed hands over a few sacks of potatoes. During a time of austerity, everyone's first priority is to eat. You will want to bear this in mind when planning for the future.

It is essential that you do not sink all your money in illiquid assets which may prove worthless when you need them. Protect your wealth by diversifying your assets and keeping a major part of it in gold.

11

DEFLATION-PROOFING
YOUR INVESTMENTS

I wonder if I should put *all* my money into gold?

Absolutely not. Gold can protect you against runaway inflation, but if a depression lies ahead, there is another form of savings you will need.

What is that?

This may sound strange, but you will want to hold dollars.

Dollars? After all you've said about inflation, I'm afraid I could lose my savings within a few years. Isn't that what you've been telling me?

If your money is in a conventional bank or savings account, inflation could make it worth less and less each year. Even if you put it someplace where it earns high interest, you will have to pay tax on whatever interest you earn. After taxes you will still be losing money. You need to find a shelter where your dollars can earn interest tax-free. Then they can protect you against inflation and depression simultaneously.

Are you saying that I should buy municipal bonds?

No, we're not recommending that. Their interest may be tax-free, but if there is a depression, your money could be tied up for a long time. We do not know how many cities may declare a moratorium on repayment of their debt, or how many could default altogether.

Why should I bother with dollars if keeping them is so much trouble?

GOLD PROTECTS YOU AGAINST INFLATION.
DOLLARS PROTECT YOU AGAINST THE
POSSIBILITY OF A DEPRESSION.

If a depression hits, money will become scarce. Credit will be tight, and everyone will want cash. People who have plenty of cash on hand will be immune to the worst effects of a depression.

YOUR DOLLARS WILL BECOME WORTH MORE.

Then, even if you lose your job, you won't have trouble buying food or making payments on your home. Everyone else will be in debt, eager to get their hands on a little cash.

How can I save money, though, without having it eaten by taxes and inflation?

The government has left you an escape route. You can protect your dollar assets by placing them in a retirement account. When you do this, the money you save is not taxed, nor is the interest it earns. By channeling money into a pension plan, you can set enough aside to protect you and your family against the possibility of a depression without being overwhelmed by inflation or taxes.

But what if I need the money before I retire? What good will it do me if it's tied up in a retirement plan?

"Pension plan" is just the name the government gave to a tax shelter which allows people like you and me to set money aside without its being taxed. Just as your gold should be viewed as a long-term investment, you will want to leave the money you set aside to protect yourself against deflation untouched until you need it. If there is an emergency and you need to withdraw funds from your "retirement account," it is easy to do. You must pay a 10% penalty to the government for early withdrawal, but the rest will be treated as normal income for the year in which you withdraw it.

It sounds like I'll lose a lot of money if I do that.

Actually, you won't because the money in your account was never taxed in the first place. In addition, it was earning tax-free interest through the years.

The benefit of opening a retirement account is that your savings go to you instead of the government. The money you put into your retirement account is not taxed, and the interest is not taxed. This adds up through the years.

The more money you usually pay the government in taxes, the more you will save by opening a retirement plan. If your tax bracket is high, you have to give the government a high percentage of your earnings under our current tax laws. By opening a retirement plan, you allow your "before tax dollars" to earn interest for you.

If you need to withdraw your money during a deflationary crisis, it will probably be because you have lost your job and do not have an alternate source of income. Your tax rate would be much lower than it is now, making what you pay less. And the *value* of the dollars you have saved will be much greater due to the effects of a deflation.

What kind of pension plan can I open?

That depends on your work. If you are self-employed, you can set up a Keogh plan and invest 15% of your annual income—up to a maximum of $15,000.

I work for someone else. What should I do?

Your employer probably has a pension plan set up for you already. Ask him if it is an individual account or if all the people where you work have one account together. Find out how your money is being invested—whether it is in stocks and bonds, or in safer investments.

Even better, it may be possible to work as an independent contractor for the firm with which you are currently employed. This would provide numerous tax advantages to both you and your employer, although qualifying for this status is not always easy.

A third possibility is to open what is known as an Individual Retirement Account (IRA). With this, the most you could contribute each year would be $2,000; or $4,000 if you are married and your spouse also works. Although the amount you can contribute to an Individual Retirement Account is relatively small, the money you save could prove very useful in the event of a depression, and in the meantime it would be shielded from high taxes and inflation.

What should I do with the money I put into my retirement account? How should it be managed?

You have a number of options. Your IRA or Keogh plan will have to have a trustee. If you have your own corporation, *you* can be the trustee. The limit on how much you can contribute is also much higher than with a Keogh plan or an Individual Retirement Account.

As your own trustee, you would be in direct control of your money at all times. That is why a lot of people are incorporating themselves and their businesses. The tax benefits alone are very great. If you are unable to incorporate, however, someone else will have to serve as your trustee.

Who would that be?

You have a variety of options. Banks, savings and loans, or money market mutual funds can all serve as your trustee, depending on which you trust.

Which do you recommend?

There are two things you can do with your money that are reasonably safe. One is to invest with a money market mutual fund, which will serve as your trustee. This is especially useful when you first open a retirement account, and the amount of money you have in it is not large. For a small fee, a money market fund will administer your investment, placing your money in whatever securities they buy.

It is also possible to have a financial planning specialist serve as your trustee, so long as he is willing to invest your money in a way you feel is safe. A few banks will even perform this service—allowing you to maintain a "directed trust," in which you tell them what to buy, and they keep this separate from their own accounts. If there is such a bank in your town, you can safely take advantage of this service.

What sort of investments should I tell my trustee to make?

Your trustee should only invest in short-term IOU's which provide *safety, liquidity and yield.*

You do not want to hold any assets that might be threatened by default. That means you have to trust whomever you lend your money to. Some borrowers are more trustworthy than others. We have already seen why you do not want to invest in municipal bonds. You might not be able to get your money when you need it.

The same is true of many corporate bonds. With the economy as fragile as it is, a depression could drive many corporations into bankruptcy. Holders of corporate debt could be left high and dry, trapped in a collapsing bond market.

There doesn't seem to be much left. Where can I invest my money and reasonably expect it to be repaid?

This may seem strange, even ironic, but right now you are probably safest lending your money to Uncle Sam. If there is a depression, many banks and corporations could fail. Life insurance companies could also go under. The United States Government, however, of all the debtors in America, would probably have the best chance of pulling through. If worse came to worst, it could tax all of us to repay its debt—something you cannot say of a bank or corporation.

What if the government did default?

Then the only thing worth holding would be gold. With gold, you are not relying on anyone's promise to pay.

If the government defaults, you will be prepared because of the gold you own. But you should also prepare for a depression. That is why we recommend that you buy short-term Treasury Bills. Right now they are the safest dollar investment. They are extremely liquid and have a high yield.[1]

Treasury Bills give you flexibility. If you invest through a T-bill money market fund, you can pull your money out at any time in response to what you see happening in the marketplace.

I've heard about T-bills. Can you tell me exactly what they are?

Treasury Bills are loan certificates issued by the government in exchange for money it borrows to finance its debt. The smallest Treasury Bill you can buy is for $10,000. The maturity rate on T-bills—that is, the date on which they are paid off with interest—ranges from 13 to 52 weeks. They can be bought either directly from the United States Treasury in Washington at its weekly auction, or through a broker in your home town. If you want to buy without an agent, you simply write or call the Federal Reserve Bank nearest you and ask for a form known as a "Tender for Treasury Bills." You should return the completed form to the bank, along with a cashier's check to cover the face value of the Treasury Bill you want to purchase.

Interest rates vary from week to week. T-bills are sold at a discount: if the government is offering 10% interest on a particular issue, it will sell a $10,000 Treasury Bill for approximately $9,000. Thus, when the bill comes to maturity in one year's time, your original investment plus 10% will equal $10,000.

If you buy your T-bills directly from the government, the discount rate you receive will be the average rate offered during that particular sale. Following this sale, the Federal Reserve Bank through which you bought your bill will send you a check to cover the difference between the face value of your Treasury Bill and its discount price. When the bill matures, after 13, 26, or 52 weeks, the U.S. Treasury will send you a check for $10,000 unless you ask that your bills be "rolled over," or renewed.

You can buy T-bills in any multiple of $5,000—with a minimum investment of $10,000 by requesting a "Tender for Treasury Bills." To obtain a "Tender for Treasury Bills," call or write to "Federal Reserve Bank" at the location nearest you:

FEDERAL RESERVE OFFICES

Atlanta, Georgia 30303
(404) 231-8500

Baltimore, Maryland 21203
(301) 539-6552

Birmingham, Alabama 35202
(205) 252-3141

Boston, Massachusetts 02016
(617) 973-3000

Buffalo, New York 14240
(716) 849-5000

Charleston, West Virginia 23511
(304) 345-8020

Charlotte, North Carolina 28230
(704) 373-0592

Chicago, Illinois 60690
(312) 380-2320

Cincinnati, Ohio 45201
(513) 721-4787

Cleveland, Ohio 44101
(216) 293-9800

Columbia, South Carolina 29210
(803) 772-1940

Columbus, Ohio 43216
(614) 846-7050

Cranford, New Jersey 07016
(201) 272-9000

Dallas, Texas 75222
(214) 651-6111

Denver, Colorado 80217
(303) 534-5500

Des Moines, Iowa 50306
(515) 284-8800

Detroit, Michigan 48231
(313) 961-6880

El Paso, Texas 79999
(915) 544-4730

Helena, Montana 59601
(406) 442-3860

Houston, Texas 77001
(713) 659-4433

Indianapolis, Indiana 46204
(317) 269-2800

Jericho, New York 11753
(516) 997-4500

Kansas City, Missouri 64198
(816) 881-2000

Lewiston, Maine 04240
(207) 784-2381

379

Little Rock, Arkansas 72203
(501) 372-5451

Los Angeles, California 90051
(213) 683-8563

Louisville, Kentucky 40232
(502) 587-7351

Memphis, Tennessee 38101
(901) 523-7171

Miami, Florida 33152
(305) 591-2065

Milwaukee, Wisconsin 53202
(414) 276-2323

Minneapolis, Minnesota 55480
(612) 783-2345

Nashville, Tennessee 37203
(615) 259-4006

New Orleans, Louisiana 70161
(504) 586-1505

New York, New York 10045
(212) 791-5000

Oklahoma City, Oklahoma 73125
(405) 235-1721

Omaha, Nebraska 68102
(402) 341-3610

Philadelphia, Pennsylvania 19105
(215) 574-6000

Pittsburgh, Pennsylvania 15230
(412) 261-7910

Portland, Oregon 97208
(503) 221-5931

Richmond, Virginia 23261
(804) 649-3611

St. Louis, Missouri 63166
(314) 421-1700

Salt Lake City, Utah 84125
(801) 355-3131

San Antonio, Texas 78295
(512) 224-2141

San Francisco, California 94120
(415) 450-2000

Seattle, Washington 98124
(206) 442-1650

Utica at Oriskany, New York 13424
(315) 736-8321

Washington, D.C. 20551
(202) 452-3000

Windsor Locks, Connecticut 06096
(203) 623-2561

Can I get someone else to buy T-bills for me?

Most banks and stock brokers will purchase them for you. When you buy through a bank or brokerage firm, you receive the discount rate at which they bought the Treasury Bills, but you also pay a brokerage fee for their service.

It seems less complicated to let them handle it for me, especially if they are going to be my pension fund trustee. But now I have another problem. I don't have $10,000 to invest in a T-bill. Does that leave me out in the cold?

No. If you do not have the money or do not want to make a large investment in T-bills right now, there is another way you can get through the door. You can invest in a money market fund which specializes in U.S. Government securities. You must make an initial investment of $1,000; but that is all. The fund will then pay you interest commensurate with the interest they receive on the Treasury Bills they hold, minus a 1% charge for operating expenses.

If you have less than $10,000 or $20,000 to invest in T-bills, this is probably the safest, easiest way to do it. The fund you choose may serve as trustee for your pension plan, protecting your dollar investment from inflation and taxes until you need it, or until the crisis facing our nation has passed.

You want to be careful not to invest in a money market fund that holds securities you would not buy yourself. Most funds are heavily invested in corporate or municipal bonds, or they have lent money to banks. They can afford to pay interest 1 or 2% higher than funds which have only government securities because they receive higher interest on their loans. We feel, however, that this higher interest does not compensate you for the risk you would be taking with your money— especially since your dollars are meant to protect you against the possibility of deflation. In the event of a depression, you want to have immediate access to your money, which can be "guaranteed" only with government securities.

Listed below are two money market funds which invest only in short-term government securities:

CAPITAL PRESERVATION FUND
755 Page Mill Road
Palo Alto, California 94306
(800) 227-8380
(800) 982-6150 (in California)
$1000 minimum investment

MERRILL LYNCH GOVERNMENT FUND
125 High Street
Boston, Massachusetts 02110
(800) 225-1576
(617) 357-1460
$5000 minimum investment

I see that if I follow your advice, I can protect myself against hyperinflation and deflation. What if neither of these happen, though? What if we muddle along and things eventually get better? Where will I be then, with all my money tied up in gold and Treasury Bills?

We are not advising you to put all your money in gold and T-bills. We just want you to cover all bases, since runaway inflation and depression are real dangers facing us today. In the event of a soft landing, gold may not be your best investment unless we return to a gold standard. The money you hold in T-bills, however, will retain its value or even appreciate as the dollar is able to buy more. When the crisis has passed, you'll be way ahead because you have saved so much money.

The overall principle governing investment in a stable economy is to let your money work for you by investing in a productive enterprise. By owning stock, anyone can be part-owner of a company that is making lots of money. Unfortunately, today's economic climate makes it difficult to invest your money in a productive way. Because of high taxes, inflation, and extreme government regulation, productivity and profits have fallen among most large American corporations. Many companies are burdened with massive short-term debt, making them particularly vulnerable to depression, with its accompanying threat of widespread bankruptcy.

If there were a soft landing, however, and a lightening of the burden of government tax and regulation on American business, the stock market could soar. For this reason, you may want to keep some of your assets in shares of common stock—investing in companies which would benefit most noticeably from an improved economic climate.

How do I know which ones they would be?

It is hard to know in advance. Even people who make a living providing others with financial advice seldom pick the winners in advance. This is shocking, but true. Of the top 3500 investment managers in this country, *the majority barely break even with their client's money*. Even the few who get a good return are seldom consistent. They may do well one year, and poorly over the next two or three.

In order to do well in the stock market, you must be able to weigh all the factors involved in an investment decision. That takes a lot of time—and ability. Few people have the talent it takes to be successful in this line of work.

Before making an investment decision about stock, you must do extensive research and think things through very carefully.

What kind of research?

You need to know:

- What a company is selling;
- Where it gets its raw materials;
- Whether its supplies are scarce or subject to disruption;
- Whether its management is flexible or rigid;
- What its labor force is like;
- Whether any labor problems could arise;
- Who its customers are;
- What future demand for its product will be;
- Whether it is part of an expanding market;
- How much competition it has; and
- Whether pressure from its competitors is likely to increase.

Do you have the time to do this kind of research? And assuming you did have the time, do you have the talent? If so, you should be a financial advisor yourself, *because hardly anyone else does!*

When you make a mistake in the stock market, you are not simply dropping a few balls. Your savings are going down the drain.

Because it is so easy to lose money in the stock market, it makes sense to let a professional invest for you. You need someone with a good track record—someone with the proven ability to pick winners year after year.

Don't I have to have a lot of money to hire someone like that?

Many investment managers will not accept accounts of less than $100,000. There is a way around this, however. You can invest in a mutual fund where your money is pooled with that of others and managed as a single account. The principle is similar to that of a money market fund: if you do not have enough money to buy a T-bill, you can open a money market account and buy a piece of one, along with many other investors.

You can lessen the risk of investing in the stock market by joining a mutual fund. It will invest in many different companies, so that any losses will easily be offset by other, appreciating stocks, providing you have a good manager. The work, skill and intelligence that go into making successful investment decisions will be his, so that you can devote your energy to other things.

What sort of fund should I choose? Which have the best managers? Do different funds have different investment philosophies?

Yes, they certainly do. Some are conservative, buying only blue chip stocks. Others focus on smaller companies with significant growth potential. We suggest you join the latter type fund, but be careful to choose one which has *proven* its ability to pick companies geared to the demands of a changing market.

Do you have any suggestions?

Yes, we recommend several mutual funds. All are "no-load" funds.

What does that mean?

There is no commission charged when you buy or sell shares of the fund. Your profit is left intact, rather than being paid to a broker, as would be the case if you bought the stock yourself.

MUTUAL FUNDS

COLUMBIA GROWTH FUND
1301 S.W. 5th Street
P.O. Box 1350
Portland, Oregon 97207
(503) 222-3600

EXPLORER FUND
P.O. Box 2600
Valley Forge, Pennsylvania 19482
(215) 648-6000

JANUS FUND
789 Sherman Street
Denver, Colorado 80203
(303) 837-1774

TWENTIETH CENTURY SELECT INVESTORS
605 West 47th Street
Kansas City, Missouri 64112
(816) 531-5575

We are recommending these funds on the basis of their past performance. There is no guarantee, however, that they will continue to perform well once *you* have invested in them. For that reason and because market conditions are constantly changing, we suggest you consult *Weisenberger's Investment Companies Service*, which you can find in most public libraries. In that way, you will be able to check current performance and dividend records for all mutual funds in the United States and thus decide which one to invest in now.

If so much profit can be made in stocks, why shouldn't I invest more of my money there?

Once we have solved our economic problems, that will be a good idea. At that point, safety will no longer be your prime consideration. Financial safety is characteristic of any stable economy.

UNTIL THEN, HOWEVER, YOU MUST BE CAREFUL OF WHAT YOU DO WITH YOUR ASSETS. YOU DO NOT WANT TO LEAVE YOURSELF VULNERABLE TO LOSS, AS YOU WOULD BE IF THERE WERE A DEPRESSION AND YOU OWNED A LOT OF STOCK. CAPITAL PRESERVATION IS THE NAME OF THE GAME RIGHT NOW. YOU WANT SAFETY, LIQUIDITY, AND ONLY THEN, YIELD.

Then, I should take steps to protect myself regardless of what happens with the economy. But how should I spread out my money? How much gold should I buy? How much silver? How much real estate should I own? How much money should I put into T-bills? How much do I want to keep in stock?

We can provide you with general guidelines, but the final decision is up to you. We simply recommend that you be comfortable with whatever you decide to do.

Don't make investment decisions that leave you feeling anxious or unable to sleep at night.

What are these guidelines you mentioned? Would you give them to me?

Your investment decisions will be influenced, among other things, by how much money you have. For example, if you have $100,000 to invest, you have more options to consider than a person with $3,000 in savings. In both cases, though, the foundation of your savings will be the same:

> GOLD TO PROTECT YOU AGAINST INFLATION, AND DOLLARS INVESTED IN A T-BILL OR T-BILL MONEY MARKET ACCOUNT TO SHIELD YOU FROM A DEPRESSION.

For example, a person with $3,000 in savings might invest $1,250 in gold coins, $250 in silver coins, and the remaining $1,500 in a money market fund which buys only Treasury securities. A person with more money might branch out into stocks, real estate (owning the property in which they live), or foreign currency.

If you are fortunate enough to have an investment manager whose judgment and ability you trust, there are many other investments he or she can make. But if you don't have access to such advice, we suggest you keep your holdings within the following range as a percentage of your net worth:

Hard money assets *Gold and silver*	**20% to 50%**
Dollar assets *Cash, T-bills,* *money market funds*	**20% to 50%**
Other *Stock, real estate, etc.*	**5% to 35%**

Once your money is properly invested, you can relax. You can enjoy life while your investments shield you and your family from the various dangers that threaten our economy.

We should remind you that gold is a long-term investment. Its price is influenced by many factors, some of which change daily. Selling out of necessity is a sure-fire way to lose money in gold.

Therefore, you will want to have a contingency fund with three to six months' living expenses in cash for sudden emergencies, preferably in a money market account. *This money should not be part of your pension plan.* It should be separate so that you can spend it without breaking into and dissolving your retirement account.

Should I save the money for this contingency fund first, before I buy any gold?

No. You should buy gold and build a cash reserve at the same time. Then, once your contingency fund covers three to six months' living expenses, you can continue buying gold and invest in a pension plan.

By diversifying your assets in this way, you reduce the risk of confronting financial disaster. By investing wisely now, you will be prepared for the future, whatever it may bring.

NOTES

1. Although we have criticized the government repeatedly for its massive spending and budget deficits, we also recognize that today's volatile economy discourages productive investments. Rather than risking your hard-earned money, right now it would be better to protect yourself and your savings so that you will have something to invest when the economic climate in this country changes.

12

GAINING CONTROL
OF YOUR LIFE

Even though I understand how to manage my money now, I still feel uneasy. I think something more is needed to cope with whatever lies ahead.

You're right. You will need a number of things besides knowing how to invest your money.

Such as?

Inner stability. Happiness. Peace of mind. You will also need a definite sense of purpose and direction. You cannot afford to continue drifting if you want to cope effectively and take advantage of the opportunities offered by the changes that lie ahead.

**I don't get enthused about my work, but I make a good living. Why do I
have to worry about where I'm going?**

If you're not going where you want to go, something is wrong. It may
not be such a problem when our economy is prosperous. But with the
financial situation as unstable as it is now, we may be in for rough
weather.

If a storm hits, you could get lost at sea unless you have a clear sense of direction. You will only find your way home if you develop the right attitude towards life.

What is this right attitude?

You need to view everything that comes your way as an opportunity for growth, although this will require a great deal of flexibility on your part. This involves being open, willing to learn, and ready to let go of the past. With the right attitude, you can learn from every aspect of your life and continue to move ahead.

Let's get down to earth. What if I lose my job? Am I supposed to be happy about that? I've got a family to support, you know.

You have been telling us in many ways that you do not like your job. Isn't that right? But right now, you're not doing anything about it. If you were forced to look for other work, you might actually find something you enjoy.

That's true.

Even if the change were forced and sudden, it could create a better life for you. If you have the right attitude, even a crisis situation can bring positive change into your life.[1]

This is called

Imagine you had to abandon your old line of work.

Rather than panic, it would be better to regain your balance quickly.

If you recognize your abilities and confidently gravitate towards a new line of work you enjoy...

you will have the opportunity to unfold much more of yourself than when you were locked into your old job.

I hope I can be that flexible. It's a tall order.

We know that. If there is an economic crisis and a temporary fall in our standard of living, many people will panic instead of taking concrete steps to solve their problems.

Most people would rather make excuses than take responsibility for their lives. This is why the government has become so large in recent years.

The tragedy is that even if we do receive government aid, it is far less than we could earn by taking care of ourselves. It's like settling for crumbs when we could enjoy a banquet.

What do you mean?

Each of us has the ability to produce wealth.[2] We all have the ability to *give* as well as to receive,[3] and at a deeper level, this is much more satisfying. Each person has a unique gift to offer to other people and the world. Once you discover what your gift is, you will know what kind of work to do.[4] And when you are determined to do what you want, nothing will stand in your way.[5]

You cannot control *all* the forces in your environment, but you can gain control of the most important person in your life.

Who is this most important person?

409

Me?

Yes, you! Your attitude towards yourself and your environment is your responsibility. Only you can control the direction of your life.[6] When you gain control of yourself, you can achieve any goal you set for yourself —even if there is confusion all around you.

Sometimes you cannot change what happens in your environment, but you are completely responsible for how you face what comes to you. Any situation can be an opportunity for growth if you use it the right way.

Many of us don't realize how powerful our thoughts are in determining the direction of our lives. The way you think determines what you attract from the world. It is as though your mind becomes a magnet and sets up a magnetic field to attract what you are thinking.[7]

If you constantly focus on problems, obstacles, and difficulties, your thoughts will hinder you in the pursuit of your goal. However, if you always see yourself getting what you want out of life, you will see opportunities all around you. You will find that what you are looking for spontaneously comes your way.

Because our thoughts are so powerful, it is essential that your mind be your friend instead of your enemy. If you use the power of your thinking in pursuing your goals, your mind will be your most important ally.[8]

"If we think of defeat, that is what we get.

If we're undecided,
then nothing will happen for us.

We must pick something great to do, and do it.

Never think of failure at all,
for as we think now, that is what we get."

You must shift your attention to the positive—to plans for achieving what you want in life. Once you focus on a goal and begin to move toward it, there will be no room in your mind for fear or doubt.[9]

Does this mean I have to be clear about what I want?

If you want to prosper in the years ahead, you must begin to set concrete goals for yourself.

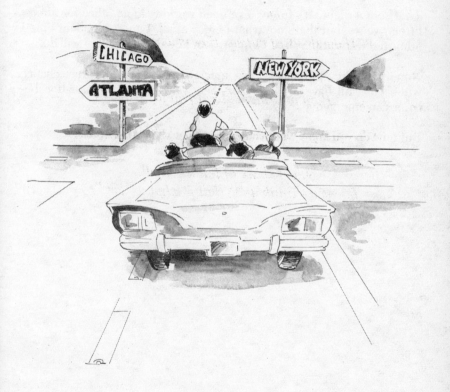

You can only reach your goal if you know where you want to go.[10]

If we experience difficult times in the future, it will be more important than ever to have concrete goals in your life. People who are drifting will feel the economic problems much more than those who are focused on achieving specific goals.

If, on the other hand, you are working towards a constructive goal, you will experience internal stability and satisfaction—even if there is confusion all around you. If you know that regardless of what happens you will eventually reach your goal, you will not lose perspective in the storm.

That seems right. It's funny. I've been working in an office for almost fifteen years, but that's not what I enjoy at all. I guess it's about time I admitted the truth. Still, if I lose my job, I don't know what I will do.

Now is the time to find out. It is much easier to make a career change while you still have a job, rather than waiting until the situation becomes an emergency.

But how do you know what your new career should be?

Because of your particular abilities, some kinds of work come naturally to you. In fact, you probably find such work so effortless and enjoyable that you do not even think of it as work, even if it is something other people consider useful.

THIS IS AN IMPORTANT CLUE TO WHAT YOU SHOULD BE DOING WITH YOUR LIFE.

Perhaps the first goal you should set for yourself is to discover what kind of work you enjoy. After all, the best way to be satisfied with your job is to do something you love.

It is not enough just to work for money. When your job fits your natural abilities and desires, you become inspired and productive. It also becomes more fun to be alive.

This establishes a strong, constructive pattern in your personal life too. Soon it becomes easy for you to accomplish *all* of your goals, whatever they may be.

I would like to find a job I enjoy, and I'm sure my friends would too. But I'm confused. I have one friend who doesn't like to do anything but go fishing. He works in a supermarket all week long and spends every weekend out on his boat. What would you say to a person like him?

There are two things we can say. First of all, if he really likes being out on the water, maybe he should change jobs. There are a number of things he could do for a living that would keep him outdoors or on a boat.

The second possibility is that there may be other areas in himself that he hasn't yet explored. Perhaps there are many things he could do, but he just hasn't looked at them yet.

The strongest thing holding most people back is their lack of imagination. They may be unsatisfied with their present situation, but they never ask themselves what would make them happy.

I wonder why not.

Most people are afraid to dive into the unknown. They do not want to take a chance and risk failure.

Too many people spend their lives doing work they don't enjoy.

But that's the way it's always been.

That's only because people cannot imagine doing something they would enjoy.

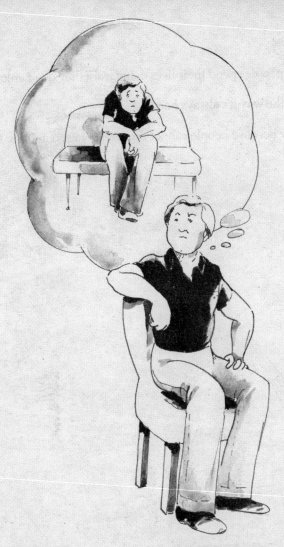

People tend to underestimate themselves. They think they are smaller than they really are. Few people ask themselves what they truly want out of life because they assume it is impossible to get it. Even fewer try to achieve what they want out of fear they will be disappointed.

Obviously, there would be no problem letting go of an old job if you knew you could find a better one somewhere else. Fear of the unknown and lack of confidence prevent people from accepting change. It would be far better to work to create the life you want to live.

I admire people who have the courage to go for what they want. I have a friend who is in the roofing business. For years, he had always worked for other people. Then, about eight months ago, he began to work for himself. He had always wanted his own business, and now that he has it, I've never seen a more enthusiastic person. When he comes over to visit us, his energy and enthusiasm inspire everyone!

It sounds like your friend believes in himself. Most people are afraid to hope for the best because they fear they will be disappointed. They don't realize that when you go for what you really want, with persistence and determination, it is not possible to fail in the long run.

But isn't failure sometimes inevitable?

Not if you set reasonable goals for youself and persist in your efforts to achieve them. If your first plan doesn't work out, come up with another one. The important thing is that you don't give up until you have reached your goal. People who refuse to accept failure usually get what they want out of life.[11]

You know, you're right. A few years ago my friend had tried to start his own business, but it didn't get off the ground. When the business failed, he had to work on someone else's crew for a while, but he never lost sight of his goal. He studied the mistakes he made and learned what he could from the experience. After a few years he tried again, and this time his business is taking off.[12]

That's good to hear. Your story reminds us of one of our business associates who is developing a new technology for solar energy. During the oil embargo in the early seventies, he felt it was important not to depend on the political system of another country for fuel. He designed and built a house for himself and his family that derived almost all of its energy from the sun.

Soon, he had a vision of making our entire nation energy self-sufficient. For a number of years, he has been moving toward this goal in practical ways. Sometime in the near future, he will start a company to manufacture solar panels and make them available to home owners at prices they can afford. His product should pay for itself in a short time through reduction of heating and electricity bills.

That sounds like a great idea to me! My heating bills were outrageous last winter!

The point here is that people should explore their fantasies, imagination, and dreams. You should try to picture yourself doing everything you have ever wanted to do, and then seriously think about doing these things. If you are not completely happy with your life as it is, you should start moving in a direction to fulfill your desires. Once you start doing things you enjoy, it is hard to go back to a job that is not suited to your nature or your abilities.

All of us have much more inside us than we ever use. It's exciting to realize what our full potential is. It is even more exciting to start using it. Once we do, we begin to enjoy both wealth and freedom.

This is exciting. But let's talk about me for just a minute. Although I don't like my job, I don't have any idea what I want to do with myself, or what direction my life should take.

There are a number of techniques you can use to get more in touch with yourself, your abilities, and your desires. To begin with, you can ask yourself a series of questions which will make your inner direction more clear.

If you have the questions, I'm ready. Start asking.

- First of all, what sort of things do you enjoy doing?[13]

- What kind of work comes easily and naturally to you?[14]

- Is there any kind of work you have done—either professionally or as a hobby—which people have said you are really good at?[15]

- Is there anything you have secretly wanted to do but were afraid to admit to yourself and your family because you thought it was not possible?[16]

You know, I do have a secret dream. For the past fourteen years, I've been working in an office, but I have always enjoyed carpentry much more. After our children were born, I built a whole extension to our house, and a few years ago I built a greenhouse in the backyard. I grow almost all my own vegetables—even in the winter.

Have you ever thought about doing carpentry for a living?

No, I haven't thought about that before. Right now, talking with you, I can't imagine why. The idea is so exciting. I should tell you about my latest hobby. Do you know anything about geodesic domes?

Probably not as much as you do.

My brother-in-law has some land in the middle of the state, but he hasn't been able to afford to build a house on it for the past several years. One weekend we were talking about his problem. He knows how much I love carpentry, and he thought I might be able to help him in some way.

Maybe this was a coincidence, but I had just read an article by Buckminster Fuller about geodesic domes, and it seemed the perfect solution to my brother-in-law's problem. Housing is the only major business in America that has not been industrialized. It takes months to build a home, and it costs a fortune.

People probably think that's the way it has to be.

They do! But then, people used to say the same thing about cars. When Henry Ford decided to mass-produce the Model T, everyone told him it was impossible. Cars had to be assembled individually, by hand. They said you could never produce thousands of cars a day in a single factory.

In the past fifteen years, there has been a similar transition in the housing industry.

A number of companies now manufacture the external shell of single family homes. The parts are packaged and shipped to a building site where they can be assembled in just a few days. It's fantastic!

After doing some research, we saw how energy efficient most of these houses are and how nice they look. A geodesic dome made of wood blends right into the environment, and there are several models available.

When we found one my sister and brother-in-law liked, they bought it. We'll assemble the frame together, and I'll design the living space inside. I've always wanted to design a house for someone, and this seems like the perfect place to start.

When are you going to do all this?

We plan to begin the dome this summer. Using the kit will save a lot of time, and I can begin to work on the inside when that is done. Also, we'll be doing everything the right way. The house will be well insulated and powered by solar energy. We plan to put in a garden so they can grow most of their own food.

Have you ever had a garden? Even in a tiny space, you can produce more than enough food for one family. Some summers we feed half the families on our block. I'm also planning to build a solar greenhouse so they can grow food all year long. We're all excited about this project, and we're hoping they can move in sometime next year.

Have you ever thought about building domes for a living?

It's one thing when it's a hobby, but if you're counting on it to pay the bills...

Just look at yourself. You're so excited and happy right now. It's such a contrast to how you feel at work each day! Imagine how you would feel if you did something you enjoyed so much *every working day of your life*.

Imagine how your life would be if you could dare to do what you want!

Just the thought is exciting. But it would take so much preparation and work.

The house you are building for your brother-in-law is a good start. It will give you valuable experience and also a model home to show other interested people. You have a good idea here—something too valuable to waste.

You know, I have thought about doing this for other people. It's been a very quiet idea because I never thought I could do it. Now I'm beginning to change my mind.

There are so many people who want to own homes but just can't afford them. Geodesic domes would put housing within the reach of many of these people. The design is energy efficient since a dome has less surface exposed to the elements than a conventional structure. You actually save 20-30% on heating and cooling. With solar energy, people could save a lot more. I could even build custom greenhouses for people who enjoy gardening and want to save money on food.

We think you have a wonderful idea. It's a practical one since it meets a real need in society. It's also good to see that your thinking is environmentally sound. You seem to be more on the way to realizing this goal than you ever knew.

I guess you're right. This idea always has been a dream of mine, but now it's feeling more and more practical. It's so exciting to think about actually doing something that was only a dream.

You will be even more excited when you do it. We all have our dreams, but most of us give up on them too easily.

That's been me alright!

If more people would get in touch with their dreams and desires, and decide they want to live them, we would have a very different world. People would pursue work that was exciting and meaningful to them, and they would contribute more to society as a result.

What about those people who don't have any idea what they want to do? There are people like that, you know.

Did you ever hear of the word "INTUITION"?

Intuition? You must be kidding! I don't believe in that.

We're not talking about anything supernatural or mysterious. We can explain intuition to you in an understandable way if you will listen for a few minutes.

OK, go ahead.

There is a basic truth about life that more and more people are beginning to realize:

YOU ARE YOUR OWN BEST FRIEND.

Intuition is *listening* to who you really are deep inside and getting in touch with what you want. Nobody else can give you that information. Yet, the answers to all the important questions in your life are deep inside you if you will only listen.[17]

If you want to decide what kind of work to do or what to do with your life, you have to take the time to listen to yourself. This quiet listening is a powerful way to move beyond your social conditioning and fear of what you can and cannot do.

Intuition is a powerful tool to move beyond the limitations you have made for yourself.

You can think of intuition as a little voice whispering in your ear. That little voice is your own. Most people have heard it at least once or twice in their lives. By sitting and listening to that inner voice, you develop a powerful tool for growth. Intuition can be one of the most valuable tools you have for recognizing, and then getting, what you really want out of life. It can also lead to a tremendous amount of happiness.[18]

That doesn't sound so mysterious after all.

It's not. Some people consider intuition the highest form of intelligence. For centuries, great artists and scientific geniuses have been more in contact with intuition than most of us. Any new creation or discovery can only come from deep within the self. The problem in using intuition is that most people have so many thoughts and so many conversations going on inside their heads that it drowns out the quiet voice which is signaling "this is right" or "this is wrong."[19]

Even if people know what they want to do, however, they may not have confidence in their abilities. This can keep them from ever achieving what they want to do with their lives.

This is a real problem. A lot of people are convinced there is nothing they can do to improve their lives. If you ask them why, they will give you a million reasons why they are unable to change:

"I don't have enough education.[20] I don't have the support of my family.[21] I don't have the time or energy to do something new..."

As long as people believe these excuses, their lives are going to be boring. Their jobs may put food on the table, but they will not be eager to greet each new day.

Rather than focus on your weaknesses, it is much better to recognize your strengths. Make a list of all the things you can do, and all the things you enjoy doing. You will soon realize that the things you do well are those you enjoy most—and that you can do much more than you gave yourself credit for.

You may get so excited making a list of all the things you do well that your life will have to change. As you develop greater self-confidence, you will be well on the way to achieving what you want in life. You will also develop a tremendous sense of freedom.

What do you mean, freedom?

When you are confident in your ability to achieve what you want in life, you will also be free of fear. You will not be tied to your present job or to any given set of circumstances. You will be ready to adapt to change whenever necessary or desirable, and you will be free to respond to any situation in the most appropriate, productive way.

IF YOU HAVE FAITH IN YOUR ABILITIES, YOU
CAN MEET THE GOALS YOU SET FOR YOUR-
SELF. PEOPLE WHO ALLOW THEMSELVES
THE OPPORTUNITY TO CHANGE AND GROW
ALWAYS FIND THEY CAN DO MUCH MORE
THAN THEY HAD THOUGHT POSSIBLE.

Like all great men and women, each of us has a secret dream. We know inside what we want to do and achieve in life. It is by realizing these dreams that we are of greatest service to humanity.

If you have the commitment to change, grow, and leave behind the frustrations, the limitations, and the security of an old way of life; the rewards will be greater than you now imagine possible.

The key to solving our economic problems lies in each of us finding work that we enjoy. When enough Americans have made this transition, our entire society will change.

NOTES

1. Proverbs 23:7.   For as he thinks within himself, so he is.

2. Deuteronomy 8:18.   But you shall remember the Lord your God, for it is He who is giving you power to make wealth.

3. Proverbs 11:25.   The generous man will be prosperous, and he who waters will himself be watered.

4. Romans 12:6.   And since we have gifts that differ according to the grace given to us, let each exercise them accordingly.

5. Proverbs 24:16.   For a righteous man falls seven times, and rises again.

6. Proverbs 16:1–3.   The plans of the heart belong to man, but the answer of the tongue is from the Lord.

   All the ways of a man are clean in his own sight, but the Lord weighs the motives.

   Commit your works to the Lord, and your plans will be established.

7. Philippians 4:8.   Finally, brethren, whatever is true, whatever is honorable, whatever is of good repute, if there is any excellence and if anything is worthy of praise, let your mind dwell on these things.

   Proverbs 2:3–7.   For if you cry for discernment, lift your voice for understanding;

   If you seek her as silver, and search for her as for hidden treasures;

   Then you will discern the fear of the Lord, and discover the knowledge of God.

   For the Lord gives wisdom; from His mouth come knowledge and understanding.

   He stores up sound wisdom for the upright; He is a shield to those who walk in integrity.

8. Proverbs 13:12. Hope deferred makes the heart sick, but desire fulfilled is a tree of life.

   Proverbs 13:19. Desire realized is sweet to the soul.

9. Second Timothy 1:7. For God has not given us a spirit of timidity, but of power and love and discipline.

10. Proverbs 4:25–26. Let your eyes look directly ahead, and let your gaze be fixed straight in front of you.

    Watch the path of your feet, and all your ways will be established.

11. Proverbs 28:25. He who trusts in the Lord will prosper.

12. Proverbs 27:23. Know well the condition of your flocks and pay attention to your herds.

13. Colossians 3:23. Whatever you do, do your work heartily, as for the Lord, rather than for men.

14. Genesis 4:21–22. And his brother's name was Jubal; he was the father of all those who play the lyre and pipe.

    As for Zillah, she also gave birth to Tubal-cain, the forger of all implements of bronze and iron.

15. Proverbs 22:29. Do you see a man skilled in his work? He will stand before kings; he will not stand before obscure men.

16. Psalms 37:4. Delight yourself in the Lord; and He will give you the desires of your heart.

17. First Corinthians 2:11. For who among men knows the thoughts of a man except the spirit of the man, which is in him?

18. Proverbs 20:27. The spirit of man is the lamp of the Lord, searching all the innermost parts of his being.

19. Hebrews 5:14. But solid food is for the mature, who because of practice have their senses trained to discern good and evil.

20. Acts 4:13.   Now as they observed the confidence of Peter and John, and understood that they were uneducated and untrained men.

21. Proverbs 12:4.   An excellent wife is the crown of her husband.

13

CHANGING YOURSELF

It's one thing to know where you want to go, but it's another thing to get there. We've been discussing techniques to get people in touch with their dreams and help them recognize their goals. What's the next step after that?

The next step is *planning* how to reach your goal,[1] and then taking concrete steps to achieve it. If you know what you want, plan carefully, and follow through with persistence, you will achieve whatever goal you set for yourself.[2]

This is the key to success in life.

However, if you want to be successful, you must also develop certain qualities in yourself.

What are they?

You must develop all of these qualities if you want to get the most out of life.

As you grow in these qualities, you will find it easier and easier to achieve your goals.

But where do I begin?

The first step in achieving success is to decide where you want to go. The next step is developing a plan to achieve your goal.[3] There are many big talkers in the world, but if you want to be successful, you must come up with feasible plans.

When people decide to build a house, they do not go about it haphazardly. First they make a blueprint, and then they begin construction. You must do the same thing with your life.

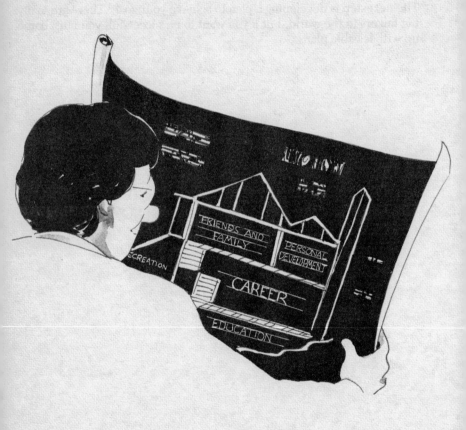

Many people I know are reluctant to move toward their goals. They may want to change, but it's hard for them to get started.

IF YOU DON'T LIKE THE WAY
YOUR LIFE IS GOING,
THERE'S NO BETTER TIME
TO CHANGE THAN RIGHT NOW.

In fact, we may all be forced to change in the years ahead. If it comes to that, however, try not to lose perspective. Even a kick from outside can sometimes get you started in the right direction.

Talking to you, it seems that people should get excited at the prospect of change. Yet my experience is that most people do not. Why is that?

In order to change, you must overcome your fears. You have to believe that the future holds something better than the present or the past. You must have confidence in yourself or in something larger than yourself. Unfortunately, few people have this kind of confidence. As a result, they cling to what is familiar rather than diving into the unknown.

OUR BIGGEST ENEMY IS FEAR.[4]

You don't try to drive with one foot on the brake and the other foot on the gas pedal. But isn't that what we are doing when we're afraid? We're trying to move ahead, yet our fears are holding us back.[5]

In addition to having a definite plan, you must overcome your fears and self-doubt. Once you develop the courage to go for what you want, you will be well on your way to success.

But how do you become courageous if you're not?

Courage is developed by walking up to what you are afraid of and facing your fears. You develop courage by forcing yourself to do things you thought you could not, and succeeding. In that way, you realize that you have more strength inside than you ever knew. You also become aware of the full extent of your inner resources. When people have the courage to put themselves in new situations, they are usually surprised by what they find they can do.

You're right about that. I remember when I was back in high school. All through my first year, I was afraid of girls. I hadn't ever asked a girl out, and I was afraid of being rejected.

How did you get over that?

I called up the girl who was driving me crazy in my geometry class and asked her out for a date. The way it turned out, she was having the same feelings about me, and she was delighted. After we went out a few times, my fears went away.

That's a good story. Instead of letting your fears control you, you were willing to confront them. Then you learned there was nothing to be afraid of.

Most people prevent themselves from trying new things because they honestly believe they cannot do anything they have never done before. They may be trapped in a job they don't like or in one that is being phased out of existence, but they still refuse to believe they can retrain for a job they would enjoy.

It sounds to me like their biggest problem is their own beliefs.

That's exactly right. If they did believe they could do something else, they certainly could.

Suppose you received a telephone call from the president of your bank, and he said that your name had been selected randomly on a computer as part of an experiment to prove that Americans can retrain to perform new jobs in a changing economy. If he said you would get one million dollars tax-free if you agreed to change careers and retrain for a job you had always dreamed of doing, you probably would not turn the money down.

Of course not!

Very few people are going to say, "Oh no, I can't do it. You can keep your million dollars."

When you are truly motivated, all your fears and excuses go down the drain. Once you focus your power and energy on achieving your goal, nothing will stand in your way.

That's a great story, but I don't know anyone who will give me a million dollars to retrain. I will have to go out on a limb if I decide to change careers. What if I don't succeed?

Right now, only fear is holding you back. You wonder if you can earn a living doing what you enjoy. The offer of a million dollars is tempting because it relieves you of that concern. Yet, if you were to serve others with enthusiasm in a field of your choice, you would probably make much more money than you do today.

It takes courage to change, but that is a small price to pay for enjoying the rest of your life and being comfortable financially. Think of the tremendous emotional rewards that will come from breaking the boundaries which have always limited what you thought you could accomplish! Think of the freedom you will feel when you discover the power within yourself to do what you want.

Sometimes it's difficult to believe in yourself, particularly if you have not yet accomplished what you want to do.

If self-confidence is a problem, *you should remind yourself again and again that you have the ability to achieve your goal*. You should also engage in persistent, continuous action directed toward its attainment. Eventually the message will sink in.[6]

You should also see that your friends[7] and family[8] support you and your desires. You will need their help if you want to achieve your goal as quickly and easily as possible.

Why is that?

It is extremely important to maintain a positive environment for yourself —both on the job and in your personal life.[9] Just as your own doubts and fears are enough to prevent you from achieving success, the doubts of others can be equally damaging.

Can you explain why?

The things other people think and feel enter your mind and tend to become a part of you. If you receive a lot of support from those around you, it will help you on your way. But if your friends and family discourage and constantly doubt you, this will require a great deal of energy to fend off.

It is important to be strong inside yourself about what you want and need, regardless of the opinions of others.[10] Nevertheless, other people do have an influence. The support of your family and friends will give you a lot more power to succeed.

How can I win their cooperation?

You can love and support them. If you deeply desire that your loved ones get what they want out of life, they are much more likely to want to help you.

If their support is not forthcoming, however, you must not allow their doubts to influence you. *You have to stay true to what is inside you.*

You want to associate with people who see themselves, and you, in terms of success, not with those who are addicted to failure. Reveal your goals only to people who will support them and expect you to succeed. It is a waste of time to tell skeptics about the great things you plan to do. People who are unhappy often laugh at the dreams of others because their own dreams have never been fulfilled.

Shouldn't I be open to constructive criticism and suggestions when I begin my work?[11]

By all means. You will have a lot to learn, and the help of others may prove invaluable. But you want to make a distinction between people who believe in you and are offering constructive advice and those who are simply being critical.

Do you have any other suggestions for building self-confidence?

The easiest way to build self-confidence is to do the best job you possibly can.[12] People who succeed take the time and effort to go the extra mile—and seek the highest level in all that they do.

It is also important to recognize that what you are doing benefits not only you, but is important to others as well. Confidence can be based on knowing the value of your contribution to your employer, your clients or to society as a whole. After all, it is easy to sell someone a product or service when you know it is the best they can buy.

Knowing that what you are doing is useful to yourself and to society will generate confidence in you—the confidence to succeed.

At first, you may need other people to encourage you to pursue your goals and your dreams. Their support can be invaluable to give you the confidence in yourself to go for what you want. Other people telling you that *you can do it* can make your own voice stronger.

The best way to become confident, though, is to do what you want to do—to know what you want, go for it, and get it. At that point, your self-confidence is deserved. By overcoming your fears and achieving success, self-confidence will develop naturally.[13]

Getting started is the hard part.

You have a point there. Most of us have something we've always wanted to do, but we think we can't do it and seldom try.

What can you do about that?

If procrastination is a problem, you can force yourself to do at least one small thing each day that will lead to the achievement of your goal. Then, try to make it two, and build up from there. But,

DO NOT LET A DAY PASS WITHOUT DOING
SOMETHING TO MAKE YOUR DREAM COME TRUE.

Gradually, you will develop a habit of engaging in dynamic activity to achieve your goals.

The secret for achieving what you want in life is putting your full attention on the steps necessary to achieve your goal. This means not allowing yourself to be distracted by the million and one things that can pull you away from it.

Time is the most precious thing in the world.[14] The moment that is lost now can never be replaced. Most people who accomplish what they want in life learn how to manage their time effectively. They do not let a day slip by without making some progress towards their goal.

But so many people don't know how to manage their time.

Then it is important for them to learn. Once you become aware of your goals, the key to success lies in working steadily to achieve them. That means making intelligent use of your time. People have developed many ways to organize their time and to structure their days usefully. Before going to bed at night, you might find it helpful to think about what you want to achieve the next day. You may even want to write it down.

I actually like to do that first thing in the morning.

It doesn't matter when you do it. The important thing is that you take the time to organize your priority of goals for the day. You should set some time aside each day—whenever you are comfortable and clear—to think about what you want to accomplish and to plan the next steps in moving towards your goal.

By organizing your time efficiently, you will develop a sense of clarity and direction. This will also help you gain control of your life.[15]

I have a friend who always makes lists of what he wants to do the next day, but then he gets so caught up doing the little picky things on his list that he never finds time to do what's really important.

If you do make lists, it's a good idea to set priorities on the things you want to do. Obviously, some things are more important than others, and the important ones deserve your first consideration. Some people find it useful to make a list of everything they want to do—in the next day, week, month, or year—and then set priorities on their goals. You can put a #1 beside the most immediate and important things you want to accomplish, a #2 beside the things which can wait for a little while, and a #3 beside things you will get to when you have some extra time. Then you can rewrite the list from time to time to incorporate new priorities.[16]

That sounds like a good idea.

Whatever method you use to organize your time, the important thing is that you do not sit around and dream.[17] Some people enjoy making lists. Other people prefer to carry around quiet intentions. However you operate, the important thing is that you always move towards your goal.

People who accomplish important things in life work hard to achieve what they want. They also enjoy their work. Because they are doing what they like and what feels natural to them, they get enthused about their work without needing outside motivation.

That's true. I find that people who are doing work they choose to do are usually enthusiastic about it.

It is natural that they should be. After all, it is easy to focus your attention and accomplish what you want when you enjoy what you do. Enthusiasm is power. It removes obstacles and wins the support of others. People respect individuals who enjoy what they do and feel strongly about their life's work. Also, inspired people inspire those around them.[18]

I've always associated these qualities with special people. But all I do is work in an office. There isn't anything special about that.

When it comes to enthusism, the line of work you do doesn't matter so long as you enjoy it. Don't you like shopping in a store where the salespeople enjoy serving you and believe in the products they are selling?

I enjoy that very much.

The enthusiasm those people have is special.

I think you are expanding my definition of what is special.

EVERYONE IS SPECIAL.
WE ALL HAVE SOMETHING USEFUL
TO OFFER THE WORLD.[19]

I guess that's true if we look inside to see what is there.

People have varied interests and abilities, and there are many important things people can do. The world is large enough that there is a meaningful place for all of us.

A while ago you mentioned cooperation. One thing I've noticed about my job is that people there don't cooperate with one another. Nobody is there to help when you need a hand. That's one of the reasons I'd like to change jobs. Things would be so much easier if we would help each other out of the tight spots we sometimes find ourselves in.[20]

Winning the cooperation of others is necessary if you want to achieve success in any field of life. Businesses where people help one another are generally far more successful than those where the employees undercut or ignore each other. When people work with, rather than against one another, a lot more work gets done. Everyone stands to profit—emotionally and financially.

But how do you win the cooperation of other people?

You win the cooperation of others by offering them what *they* want or need. Most of us think only in terms of our own desires. When two people come together thinking only of themselves, there are bound to be problems. Each is expecting to get something from the other, but *neither is willing to give.*[21]

If you want to win the cooperation of others, you must learn to go the extra mile—giving what the other person wants, in abundance. People appreciate generosity and are usually glad to return the favor.[22]

I'm afraid you're being idealistic. Most people aren't like that, you know. There are many people around who only use other people.

You certainly don't want to let people take advantage of you, but that doesn't mean you can't treat them the way you want to be treated yourself. Many people aren't ready to behave decently, but that is their problem. Don't let it be yours.[23]

Giving is reciprocal. When you help other people with what they do, they tend to be much more eager to help you. People who understand this find it much easier to get what they want out of life.

A typewriter repairman we know built a successful business because he believed in always doing the best job he possibly could. In addition to being conscientious and skilled, he had a warm personality. People felt good when they entered his store because he was always glad to see them, and they knew he was always fair in his business practices.

When he began his business fifteen years ago, he decided that he would earn his living only by fixing genuine problems. If people needed advice about typewriters or repairs, he told them what they needed for free. If a person came in with a minor problem, he would fix it for a nominal cost. But no matter how large or small any task was, he always did a good job.

In this way, he earned the trust of the community. If anyone needed to buy a typewriter, they would go out of their way to buy it from him. And because he did such excellent work on the machines he fixed, people began to bring him all of their repairs. Soon he had more business than he could handle by himself, so he hired assistants whom he taught to do business the same way he did. All of them earn a comfortable living.

I can see why people would go to him. So many people do less than adequate work, yet they expect to be paid. Most of the people where I work try to do as little as possible on the job. Sometimes I don't blame my boss for getting annoyed with them.

What those people do not understand is that they are really cheating themselves. If they produced more, they would be worth more and could command a higher salary—if not from their present employer, then from someone else who was better able to recognize their true value. There is seldom a shortage of jobs for people who are willing to offer their best to the world.

The quickest way to become rich in every way is to contribute something of value to the world.

That sounds like a fine ideal, but it's really not that way out in the world, you know.

This may not be the current business ethic, but it *is* the key to true success. In any relationship, whether business or personal, there is maximum gain whenever there is maximum giving on both sides.[25]

Some people who don't think like this are successful.[26]

In terms of money, perhaps, but not in terms of happiness or peace of mind. You cannot measure success in monetary terms alone. A ruthless businessman may accumulate a large fortune, but he may not have friends, love or happiness in his life.[27]

You must form a habit of doing the best job you possibly can in exchange for the money you receive. By doing so, you will make the world a better place to live and increase the wealth and happiness of those around you.[29]

But let me ask you now—what happens if you know what you want to do and start working towards your goal, but find that your plans are not working out?

In that case it is important that you be flexible. Figure out why your plan isn't working, make the necessary adjustments, and learn from your mistakes. You cannot possibly anticipate everything that is going to happen in the future. In pursuing your goal, it may be necessary to adjust your plans from time to time.

I find that many people are unwilling to let go of a plan once they've decided to do something a particular way.

Inflexibility is dangerous. If carried to an extreme, it will prevent you from ever achieving success. If you can be flexible, it becomes much easier to meet your goals, regardless of changing circumstances in your environment.

If you want to reach a particular
goal, you cannot afford to stop
until you get there. If you have
to change plans, then change your
plans. But keep on moving
until you succeed.

If you decide to climb a mountain, don't give up until you reach the top. Don't let anything discourage you. Once you start moving towards your goal, you will make some mistakes. We all do—it is part of the learning process. But don't give up and climb back down the mountain.[30]

Whenever things don't go as planned, you have an opportunity to learn something. As soon as you learn the lesson, you will be able to move on. If you learn from your mistakes and continue moving towards your goal, you will succeed.

Just as mistakes should never discourage you, don't be overwhelmed by temporary obstacles. We are always being tested to see how we respond to problems. Do we give up whenever we meet an obstacle?[31]

Or do we stand up to face the challenge?

If you know how to transform obstacles into opportunities, your road will be paved with success. You will know how to get what you want out of life without letting anything hold you back.

What happens if I don't get what I want right away?

Most desirable things are not acquired in an hour, or even in a month or two. What is important is that you keep on moving until you reach your goal. With the right attitude, it probably won't take as long as you might expect.

If you know what you want in life, have a sound plan, and keep moving toward your goal, nothing will stop you from fulfilling your desires. You will be in control of your life, and success will inevitably be yours.

NOTES

1. Proverbs 16:3.   Commit your works to the Lord, and your plans will be established.

2. Proverbs 13:21. The righteous will be rewarded with prosperity.

3. Proverbs 21:5.   The plans of the diligent surely lead to advantage.

4. Second Timothy 1:7.   For God has not given us a spirit of timidity, but of power and love and discipline.

   Deuteronomy 31:8.   And the Lord is the one who goes ahead of you; He will be with you. He will not fail you or forsake you. Do not fear, or be dismayed.

5. Job 3:25.   For what I fear comes upon me, and what I dread befalls me.

6. Proverbs 23:7.   For as he thinks within himself, so he is.

7. Proverbs 17:17.   A friend loves at all times, and a brother is born for adversity.

8. Proverbs 12:4.   An excellent wife is the crown of her husband.

9. Proverbs 13:20.   He who walks with wise men will be wise.

   Proverbs 27:17.   Iron sharpens iron, so one man sharpens another.

10. Proverbs 4:23.   Watch over your heart with all diligence. For from it flow the springs of life.

11. Proverbs 19:20.   Listen to counsel and accept discipline, that you may be wise the rest of your days.

12. Ecclesiastes 9:10.   Whatever your hand finds to do, verily, do it with all your might.

13. Proverbs 13:19.   Desire realized is sweet to the soul.

14. James 4:14.   Yet you do not know what your life will be like tomorrow. You are just a vapor that appears for a little while and then vanishes away.

15. Proverbs 23:12.   Apply your heart to discipline, and your ears to words of knowledge.

16. These ideas are explored in detail in Alan Lakein's *How to Get Control of Your Time and Your Life* (New York: David McKay, 1973).

17. Proverbs 14:23.   In all labor there is profit, but mere talk leads only to poverty.

18. Proverbs 22:29.   Do you see a man skilled in his work? He will stand before kings; he will not stand before obscure men.

19. Romans 12:6.   And since we have gifts that differ according to the grace given to us, let each exercise them accordingly.

20. First Peter 3:8–9.   To sum up, let all be harmonious, sympathetic, brotherly, kindhearted, and humble in spirit;

   not returning evil for evil, or insult for insult, but giving a blessing instead; for you were called for the very purpose that you might inherit a blessing.

21. Philippians 2:3–4.   Do nothing from selfishness or empty conceit, but with humility of mind let each of you regard one another as more important than himself;

   do not merely look out for your own personal interests, but also for the interests of others.

22. Proverbs 11:25.   The generous man will be prosperous, and he who waters will himself be watered.

23. Romans 12:18.   If possible, so far as it depends on you, be at peace with all men.

Matthew 7:12.   Therefore whatever you want others to do for you, do so for them, for this is the law and the prophets.

24. Proverbs 12:14.   The deeds of a man's hands will return to him.

25. Luke 6:38.   Give, and it will be given to you; good measure, pressed down, shaken together, running over, they will pour into your lap. For whatever measure you deal out to others, it will be dealt to you in return.

26. Proverbs 14:12.   There is a way which seems right to a man, but its end is the way of death.

27. James 5:1–4.   Come now, you rich, weep and howl for your miseries which are coming upon you.

Your riches have rotted and your garments have become motheaten.

Your gold and your silver have rusted; and their rust will be a witness against you and will consume your flesh like fire. It is in the last days that you have stored up your treasure!

Behold, the pay of the laborers who mowed your fields, and which has been withheld by you, cries out against you; and the outcry of those who did the harvesting has reached the ears of the Lord of Saboath.

28. Proverbs 19:17.   He who is gracious to a poor man lends to the Lord, and He will repay him for this good deed.

29. Proverbs 10:4.   Poor is he who works with a negligent hand, but the hand of the diligent makes rich.

30. Proverbs 24:16.   For a righteous man falls seven times, and rises again.

31. James 1:3.   The testing of your faith produces endurance.

14

CHANGING THE NATION

I know things need to change. That much is obvious. But I'm just one person. What can I do?

The problems our country is facing are huge. And yet, the only way we can improve things is by each of us taking responsibility for our own life. All changes in society are brought about by individuals. If large numbers of individuals—people like you and me—become more productive and self-sufficient, this will change our nation as a whole.

Don't you think the government needs to change also? You keep talking about how inflationary policies are ruining the economy and how government is subsidizing so many special interest groups. What can we, as individuals, do about that?

Our country needs a whole change of attitude. People are often so concerned with what they want and need that they lose touch with the fact that we live in a community. This attitude has caused tremendous problems for all of us. We need to broaden our horizons and realize that everything we do as individuals affects the people, the community, and the nation around us.

Instead of seeing what we can take from government, we need to be weaving productive threads into the fabric of society. We need to be as useful as possible to ourselves and to everyone else.

There are different areas of responsibility in life—those of the individual, the family, the church and government. God has designed the world in such a way that each of these responsibilities can be met in an appropriate way.

What do you mean?

To begin, with, the individual has certain responsibilities. For example, each of us is responsible for taking care of ourselves, and *not* being a burden on society. We are responsible for leading a life of love and devotion to God. And we must live according to our conscience and convictions. The more we are self-governed in this way—following the Word of God—the less we will need *external* forms of government.

What about our relationships with other people?

Self-responsibility also involves living a life of love and kindness. As Jesus said: "Thou shalt love the Lord thy God with all thy heart, and with all thy soul, and with all thy mind. This is the first and great commandment. And the second is like unto it, Thou shalt love thy neighbor as thyself. On these two commandments hang all the law and the prophets." There are opportunities to be giving every day—both in our personal lives and in our work. We were put on this planet to help and love one another, and people who are fulfilled generally find that their fulfillment grows when they share it.

What about the responsibilities of the family?

The family and its structure is a beautiful expression of God's love. When a husband and wife are devoted to one another, they form a union which is more powerful than either of the individuals were when they were alone. This relationship can form a firm ground for loving and serving God. However, with the blessings of this relationship also come its responsibilities.

Economically, the family should take care of its own. The family has a moral obligation to care for, educate, and provide for its members.[1]

Also, parents have the responsibility of passing on spiritual values to their children.[2]

Husband and wife are both servants of God. By serving society and by raising a family of self-sufficient, morally responsible, and devout children, each family does its part to create a society in harmony with God's law.

What about the church?

The responsibility of the church is to strengthen the family and the individual in their religious faith, in their moral values, in their sense of self-responsibility, and in their ability to love and serve one another as Christians. In addition, it is the responsibility of the church to provide for the needy—but only for those who are truly unable to care for themselves.[3]

Then what about government? If individuals and families are self-sufficient, and the church is performing its role of providing for those who are truly in need, what is the government supposed to do?

The basic purpose of government is to maintain law and order—by protecting the righteous and punishing wrongdoers. The biblical concept of government is limited, with families and individuals doing their share to provide for themselves and to create the life they want.

Instead of seeing what we can take from government or wanting government to assume responsibilities that we should be assuming ourselves, we should be thinking about how we can contribute to society and how we can become as productive as possible as individuals. If we can restore the proper functions of responsibility back to the individual, the family, the church, and to government; our society will return to a state of harmony with God's law, and our nation will be blessed.[4]

It seems that some people may have to give up their government jobs or refuse government handouts if we want to bring this about.

That's right. This will require a sacrifice on the part of some individuals, but this transition will make our society much stronger in the long run. If people relied on themselves and the church, there wouldn't be any need for the government to take care of them.

Also, there are real limits to how much the government can give you. What you can create for yourself is far greater.

What else can we do to get our nation back on the track?

You can encourage the President and Congress to cut government spending and balance the federal budget—by gradually eliminating all government subsidies to special interest groups. If you support this kind of change and make the most of your own life, you will make an important contribution to solving our nation's problems. Prosperity will arrive almost before you know it. *But the months and years ahead are crucial. We must act now to avoid a potential disaster.*

Is there any way that we can make the government change?

Yes, by influencing Congress. That is where the spending power of government lies.

Politicians are usually afraid to cut programs because they depend on special interest groups for campaign money and votes. They are often elected by promising government favors to their constituents. If the public turns around, however, and demands an end to this, Congress will have no choice but to go along. As politicians see individuals taking care of themselves and churches providing for those in need, many of them will *want* to return to a limited form of government.

You make it sound too easy.

You may be right. The change our nation needs will require a sacrifice on the part of many individuals.

That could be uncomfortable.

It may be for a while, but it is important to keep in mind that this period of transition is only *temporary*. We have to change and sacrifice now because some bad decisions were made in the past. It will take some time to overcome them, and it will take courage. What we should keep in mind is that the sacrifice we make at this time will bring us far greater prosperity in the future.

That sounds worthwhile to me. But do you think the American people have courage? Courage is something we have all read about, but it's not something I see in many people today.

The American people have a tradition
of courage. It is something inside
all of us, and something we can draw
forth when we need it.

Let me tell you a story. My daughter goes to a small university in Iowa. A few winters ago during the energy crisis, there was a shortage of fuel to heat the campus. The president of the university called a meeting of the entire student body and told them that the fuel supply to the campus was about to be cut drastically. He explained the situation to them in great detail, telling them what kind of sacrifice would be necessary to keep the campus open. Then, he asked the students themselves to decide whether they wanted to close the campus for several weeks until the crisis was over or make the sacrifices that would be necessary to continue classes.

What did they do?

They decided to keep the campus open. For several weeks during the coldest winter in years, everyone had to keep the heat below 60 degrees during the day, and even lower at night. There was no hot water for three weeks, and they could only turn it on for brief intervals for some time after that.

It sounds terrible.

Actually, it was not. The students banded together with a pioneer spirit and decided to go through the crisis as a group adventure. Instead of complaining about the situation and feeling sorry for themselves, they cooperated during the hard times. People shared electric teapots when they had to wash their hair, and men used Coleman stoves when they wanted to shave. One night when it was way below zero with the wind-chill factor, they had a dance to keep warm. My daughter has fond memories of that winter because the whole community banded together with such warm feelings and so much courage.

I can see what you are saying. If we Americans face the coming transition with the right attitude, I'm sure it will be much easier.

When a time of crisis comes, you have to use your inner resources. Many people will find they are much stronger than they ever realized. And by working together, we can pass through the transition period as quickly and smoothly as possible.

The basis of inner strength, of course, is firm faith in God. If you trust in God, He will strengthen you and give you the inner resouces to meet the changes that lie ahead.[5]

That's very encouraging. Still, how can we change the government? Special interests are firmly entrenched in this country. You yourself have described how politicians depend on these groups for support. I'm just one person. It is hard to believe there is anything I can do to improve the quality of our government.

Special interest groups depend on
people like you to keep quiet
while they use the government
to their advantage.
If you speak up and make
your voice heard in Washington,
power will begin to shift
your way.

Are you sure? I thought politicians vote the way special interests tell them to.

If special interest groups give money to your Congressman, he may vote the way they want. The only reason this can happen, though, is because many people do not vote, and those who do are often uninformed. In the last general election, only 53% of the population voted. Worse yet, only 26% of professing Christians voted—when they, of all people, should know God's principles and should be responsible for ensuring righteousness in government. *By being informed and voting, you will influence what your Congressman does.*

Also, you should never just listen to any politician without educating yourself about where he stands on the issues that are important to you—even if he comes to your church with a Bible in his hand. Check his voting record. See if he has voted in accordance with his convictions or whether he has been swayed by special interest groups. See if he has kept his campaign promises or whether he has changed after getting into office. Politicians know that if they don't keep their voters happy, they will lose their jobs.

> ONCE POLITICIANS REALIZE THEY CANNOT SERVE
> SPECIAL INTERESTS WITHOUT LOSING THE NEXT
> ELECTION, THEY WILL CHANGE THEIR TUNE.

What do you suggest I do?

FIRST OF ALL, VOTE IN EVERY ELECTION.

YOU CAN ALSO WRITE POSTCARDS TO YOUR SENATORS AND CONGRESSIONAL REPRESENTATIVES. Even a few lines saying which policies you want your representatives to support will make a difference!

What should I say?

Say what you feel.

- That you want to see the federal budget balanced immediately!

- That you want the United States to return to a full gold standard. No partial standard which leaves room for inflation will do.

- That you want to end all government subsidies for special interest groups.

- Then, as government spending falls, taxes should be reduced.

That sounds easy enough. Where should I send my postcards after I write them?

Send them to your representatives in Washington. You can reach your Congressman or Congresswoman at the following address:

> Name of Representative
> House Office Building
> Washington, D.C. 20515.

Your Senators' mail should be sent to the following address:

> Name of Senator
> Senate Office Building
> Washington, D.C. 20510.

You can also write the President and members of his cabinet, such as the Secretary of the Treasury:

> President of the United States
> The White House
> Washington, D.C. 20500
>
> Secretary of the Treasury
> Department of the Treasury
> Washington, D.C. 20520.

Once you have written your postcards, you can mail them, one per week, to your Senators, Congressional Representatives, and the President of the United States. Also, be sure to include your return address. The impact of your writing will be important.

Are you sure it will have an effect?

Mail to your elected representatives does make an impression because they depend on you for their votes. If you send them postcards week after week, they will realize that the public is serious. Their job depends on how well they respond to what the public wants.

Sometimes it doesn't take as much mail as you would expect to make an impression. In 1980, a Congressman from the Midwest was planning to vote for another large spending bill. Suddenly, he changed his mind and cast his vote the other way. When asked why he had switched his vote, the Congressman said he had heard from his constituents that they were opposed to the bill.

How many letters had he received?

Ten.

You must be kidding!

Policitians realize that for each person who feels strongly enough to write on any given issue, there are usually *ten thousand* people who agree but have not bothered to express their feelings.

This is why taking the time to write your elected representatives is so important. If large numbers of Americans—people like you and me—would take the time to express their feelings, *we could turn this country around overnight,* and bring our nation back to God.

Our purpose as Christians is to bring glory to God in all things.[6] This requires that we as individuals and as a nation be good stewards of all that God has given to us. Among other things, this includes making certain that our government, our economy, and our legal system are structured in accordance with biblical principles. Unfortunately, most of us have been so involved with our own lives that slowly, over the years, we have forgotten to ensure that our government, our schools, and our social organizations are structured along these lines.

It is our responsibility, as Godly people, to see that the principles of God's Word are applied in all areas of government. If we will not stand up for God's righteousness and His principles, who will? If we will not perpetuate the biblical character of the men and women who founded this great nation, who will? And if the scriptures require that wickedness be taken out of government, and we don't know how or don't have the time, who will?[7]

All we are talking about is spending ten minutes a week writing postcards and mailing them regularly to Washington. It's a small price to pay if it will help preserve our freedom and financial security.

I'm going to stop by the post office and pick up some postcards tomorrow. But let me ask you one thing. What if my Congressman doesn't change, despite the letters he receives?

Then you will have to vote him out of office next November. Your future and the future of your country are at stake.[8]

We must elect men and women who refuse to support special interests, who believe in limited government, who believe that government should be structured in accordance with biblical principles,[9] and who want to promote the welfare of *all* Americans by getting our economy on the track once again.

Things cannot go on the way they have much longer. God will bring increasing pressure to bear on us until we see the need to return to His principles. The time has come to change and become a nation of self-sufficient people.

By undergoing this change yourself, you will soon enjoy greater prosperity than you ever dreamed was possible—and do your share to bring about a great transformation of American society.

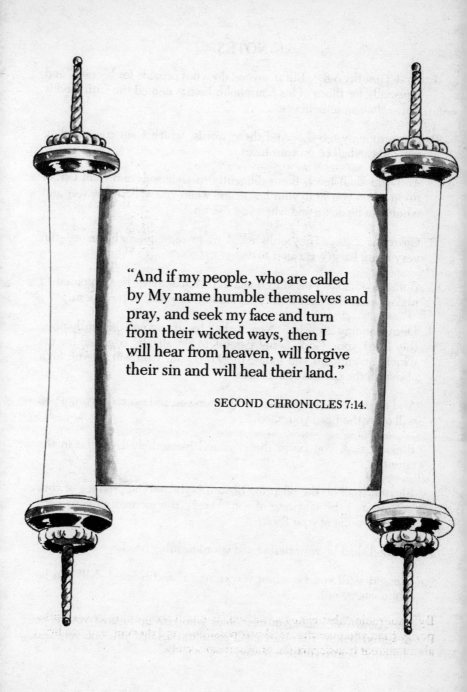

"And if my people, who are called by My name humble themselves and pray, and seek my face and turn from their wicked ways, then I will hear from heaven, will forgive their sin and will heal their land."

SECOND CHRONICLES 7:14.

NOTES

1. First Timothy 5:8. But if anyone does not provide for his own, and especially for those of his household, he has denied the faith, and is worse than an unbeliever.

2. Deuteronomy 6:6–7. And these words, which I am commanding you today, shall be on your heart;

   And you shall teach them diligently to your sons and shall talk of them when you sit in your house and when you walk by the way and when you lie down and when you rise up.

3. Galatians 2:10. They only asked us to remember the poor—the very thing I also was eager to do.

   Romans 15:26. For Macedonia and Achaia have been pleased to make a contribution for the poor among the saints in Jerusalem.

4. Deuteronomy 28:1–14. Now it shall be, if you will diligently obey the Lord your God, being careful to do all His commandments which I command you today, the Lord your God will set you high above all the nations of the earth.

   And all these blessings shall come upon you and overtake you, if you will obey the Lord your God.

   Blessed shall you be in the city, and blessed shall you be in the country.

   Blessed shall be the offspring of your body and the produce of your ground and the offspring of your beasts, the increase of your herd and the young of your flock.

   Blessed shall be your basket and your kneading bowl.

   Blessed shall you be when you come in, and blessed shall you be when you go out.

   The Lord will cause your enemies who rise up against you to be defeated before you; they shall come out against you one way and shall flee before you seven ways.

The Lord will command the blessing upon you in your barns and in all that you put your hand to, and He will bless you in the land which the Lord your God gives you.

The Lord will establish you as a holy people to Himself, as He swore to you, if you will keep the commandments of the Lord your God, and walk in His ways.

So all the peoples of the earth shall see that you are called by the name of the Lord; and they shall be afraid of you.

And the Lord will make you abound in prosperity, in the offspring of your body and in the offspring of your beast and in the produce of your ground, in the land which the Lord swore to your fathers to give you.

The Lord will open for you His good storehouse, the heavens, to give rain to your land in its season and to bless all the work of your hand.

5. Philippians 4:13.   I can do all things through Him who strengthens me.

6. First Peter 4:11.   Whoever speaks, let him speak, as it were, the utterances of God; whoever serves, let him do so as by the strength which God supplies; so that in all things God may be glorified through Jesus Christ, to whom belongs the glory and dominion forever and ever. Amen.

7. Matthew 5:13.   You are the salt of the earth; but if the salt has become tasteless, how will it be made salty again? It is good for nothing any more, except to be thrown out and trampled under foot by men.

8. Proverbs 25:5.   Take away the wicked from before the king, and his throne will be established in righteousness.

9. Second Corinthians 3:17.   Now the Lord is the Spirit; and where the Spirit of the Lord is, there is liberty.

APPENDIX

TESTIMONY BEFORE THE U.S. GOLD COMMISSION

by

Murray N. Rothbard

Professor of Economics
Polytechnic Institute of New York

November 12, 1981
Washington, D.C.

In recent years, economists and other analysts have come more and more to see the errors and fallacies of government control and central planning, and the great importance of maintaining the rights of private property and of free markets and free enterprise. But while the economics of the free market and property rights has been extended in recent decades, there is one glaring gap: the crucial area of money.

Why are we ready to accept freedom and private property, why are we ready, in short, to trust the people in all their economic affairs—and yet make a glaring exception in the case of money? Why do we favor freedom in many areas, and yet advocate placing total control over the supply and lending of money in the hands of the central government?

For if we leave it up to the federal government to control the issue of dollars and demand liabilities to dollars, we are granting it this vital power. Money is relevant to the lives of every American. And yet we are willing to put our lives and our fortunes, if not perhaps our sacred honor, in the hands of the Federal Reserve, the monopoly creator and controller of all dollar issues.

It might be well for us to ponder how perhaps the most despotic regime of this century—Pol Pot's Cambodia—was able to exercise its genocidal policies over the Cambodian people. It did so by abolishing all use of money, so that no one could use money to purchase goods, and everyone had to go to the central government to receive their meagre rations of food or clothing. The point here is not that I think that the Federal Reserve policies rank with Pol Pot's—only to underscore the vital importance to everyone's life of the people directing the control of their nation's money rather than the government.

Yet in the field of money we allowed the U.S. government to confiscate everyone's gold in 1933, supposedly for the duration of the depression emergency. But here we are, nearly half a century later, and the people's gold, seized from them, still remains buried at Fort Knox. If we truly believe in free markets, free people, and private property, we must proceed to denationalize gold, and let the people take back their gold property which was, in effect, stolen from them in 1933 and never returned.

But let us go back to our central question: do we trust the people, or the government? I would like to submit that it is precisely the area of money—an area nationalized throughout the world—where we cannot trust government at all, and even less so than in other areas of the economy. For government operation using taxpayer money rather than voluntary investment or payments from consumers always tends to be unsatisfactory and hopelessly inefficient. But in the area of money there is another vital factor, which causes the government to be inherently inflationary. Most economists will now concede that the major, if not the sole, cause of our chronic and ever-accelerating inflation is the excessive creation of new money. But there is only one institution to blame for this, because there is only one institution that we all recognize to be the sole issuer and controller of dollars: the federal government and particularly the Federal Reserve. But if, as I maintain, government is inherently inflationary, then putting the Fed or any other government institution in charge of the supply of money is equivalent to letting the proverbial fox guard the chicken coop.

Why do I say that government is inherently inflationary? Simply because government, like many of the rest of us, is chronically short of funds—that is, it would like to spend more than it can take in in taxes without stirring up too much political unrest. To pay for the remainder, it can borrow from the public, or better yet, it can create new money and use it to finance its ever-larger deficits. The point is that economically, if not legally, the federal government—now the Federal Reserve—enjoys the monopoly of legalized counterfeiting, of creating new money out of thin air, or out of paper and ink. I submit that any institution, no matter how noble its possible motives, will use any power that it has, especially the power to counterfeit. By creating new money, the government can finance its deficits, and subsidize favored political and economic groups by supplying cheaper credit than they would otherwise enjoy. Since the government, as monopoly issuer of fiat money, has the power and the ability to counterfeit, it will tend to keep using such power.

If we look at the record of governments throughout history, we see a dismal story of such counterfeiting—of fiat money, of runaway inflation that wiped out entire classes of people as well as destroying the value of the nation's currency. There is no economic holocaust—no recession or depression—that can touch the widespread and intense agony of runaway inflation. And if we continue our present course of trusting government rather than the people or the market, we will eventually have such hyperinflation in America. Let us not forget that two of the notable runaway inflations in the twentieth century had disastrous political consequences: the German inflation of 1923 destroyed the middle class and paved the way for Hitler; and the Chinese inflation of the 1940s was instrumental in the loss of China to the Communists.

It is also unassailably true that the Western world enjoyed far greater price stability under the gold standard than we have had since. If we take the period since the founding of the American Republic, prices were far more stable than they have been since we were taken off gold in 1933. This is still more true if we realize that two of the major inflationary episodes occurred when the federal government issued fiat dollars inconvertible into gold (i.e., when we were off the gold standard): the War of 1812, when the government allowed the banks to issue dollars and not redeem them; and the Civil War, when North and South alike issued irredeemable greenbacks. And the situation improves still more if we take the pre-Federal Reserve era before 1913 and compare it with later periods, for an unmanaged gold standard with free or semi-free banking works much better and more stably than a gold standard managed—and thereafter distorted and crippled—by a central bank such as the Federal Reserve.

It is possible, though not easy, to write off this historical record of the virtues of gold and the vices of fiat paper by attributing it to coincidence and various special features in the past. But if we understand that government, as legalized monopoly counterfeiter is inherently inflationary, then we will see that the historical record is not a problem or puzzle, but simply confirms and illustrates our basic insight.

If we must denationalize gold, then we must also and at the same time denationalize the dollar—taking the issuance of dollars out of the hands of the government or the central bank. To eliminate and exorcise the spectre of inflation, we must see to it that gold, dollar, and money are in the hands of the people, of the free market, rather than the central bank. How can this be done? How can we establish freedom and private property in money, while denationalizing gold and the dollar? Only by restoring the concept of the "dollar," not as an independent entity, but what it was before 1933: simply a unit of weight of gold. That is what a "gold standard" means. But in order for the dollar to truly be a certain weight of gold, it must be redeemable on demand at that weight. Only if the average person can redeem his dollars at a fixed weight of gold coin can a true gold standard exist or perform its important functions.

This means that nothing less will do. A return to something like the Bretton Woods system, where the dollar was supposedly fixed in terms of gold but where only foreign central banks could redeem in gold, would be a sham and would only end in the same sort of disaster as did Bretton Woods in 1971. The dollar must be redeemable in gold not just to foreign governments but to everyone, Americans and foreign citizens alike. Only in this way can the dollar be tied firmly to the stable level of gold. Also it is important that gold be redeemable in coin and not merely bullion. For redeemability in bullion, such as existed in England during the 1920s and the United States from 1933 to 1971, might benefit wealthy businessmen and international operators, but it deprives the average person of the right to keep his property in gold rather than paper or deposit dollars.

It is furthermore important not to introduce escape clauses into the gold standard or to provide for changes in the definition of gold weight. A gold standard with an escape clause is useless, for it simply signals everyone that we don't really mean it, that the gold discipline to guard us from inflation won't really be enforced. Similarly with changes in definition. The gold standard is unfortunately commonly talked of as "fixing the price of gold." The gold standard, however, does not fix the price of gold in terms of dollars; rather it defines the dollar in terms of a weight of gold. Changing that definition makes as little sense, and is even more pernicious, than changing the definition of a pound from 16 to 14 ounces. Just as an "ounce" or "pound" is each a unit of weight and therefore fixed in relation to each other, so should be the dollar and a weight of gold.

But just as "pound" and "ounce" are initially arbitrary definitions and, once chosen, should remain fixed, so the initial definition of a dollar in terms of gold is also arbitrary. No one takes seriously the current statutory definition of the dollar as approximately $42 per ounce, because there is no real way in which the dollar and gold are related. We should pick the most convenient initial definition and stick to it from then on.

I suggest that the most convenient definition would be one that would truly embody the dollar as a unit of weight of gold: a 100% reserve of the gold stock to the dollars—paper money and demand deposits—outstanding. This would be approximately $1600 an ounce. This high price—or rather low weight—of gold would not be inflationary, if, as should be done, reserve requirements are 100% from that point on. In no case should higher value of the gold stock be used to pyramid more inflationary dollars on top of the gold. Furthermore, this sort of 100% gold dollar would enable the rapid liquidation of the Federal Reserve System and the establishment of sound, uninflated free banking.

There are several common criticisms of the idea of a return to the gold standard. One is that we would be relying on the fluctuations of the supply of gold production on the market. We are fortunate, however, that gold is such a durable commodity that annual production can only be a small proportion of the total stock, and will therefore have little impact on prices. This is in contrast to paper money, which can be increased at will and nearly costlessly by the central government. No one says that gold is an abstractly "perfect" money, whatever that may be. It is far more trustworthy, however, than government.

Secondly, gold has often been blamed for the severity and extent of the Great Depression of 1929 and the 1930s. We should turn that charge around and point out that the New Deal could not get us out of the depression despite taking us off the gold standard in 1933. But more important, the crash of 1929 was caused, not by the gold standard but by the unsound management of the gold standard by the Federal Reserve System. Throughout the 1920s, the Fed unwisely kept pumping inflationary money and credit into the economy in order to help Great Britain to try to get out of the severe economic problems it had gotten itself into in the 1920s. Britain had gone back to gold at an overvalued pound in the 1920s, and tried to offset the resulting deflation and inability to export by getting other countries to inflate and to return to a phony "gold exchange" standard pyramiding money on top of the English pound. The United States was induced to inflate its own money and credit in order to keep Britain from losing gold to America. The tragic result was the 1929 crash and all countries going off gold.

At the onset of the crash, President Hoover, later followed by Roosevelt, prolonged the depression indefinitely by a host of "New Deal" measures: inducing businesses to keep wage rates at pre-1929 boom levels; vast loans to near-bankrupt businesses; public works expenditures; farm price supports; budget deficits; and the rest of the by now familiar apparatus of New Deal measures.

Another criticism of gold is that the two countries most benefitting from a gold standard would be particularly unpalatable politically: South Africa and the Soviet Union, the two leading gold producing countries. But we have never balked at purchasing oil, minerals, or other important goods from politically repellent nations. Why stop at gold? Furthermore, if the United States becomes healthier economically and defeats inflation by adopting a gold standard, this would help us far more than we would be hurt from Russia's gain from a higher price of gold.

A fourth complaint is that, while an international gold standard would be acceptable, the United States could never successfully go back to gold on its own. Lengthy international negotiations and numerous conferences would need to be held before a gold standard could return. But I see no reason why the U.S. could not return to gold immediately on its own. The resulting stability and end to inflation would set a superb example for foreign nations. I am sure that such hard money countries as Switzerland, France, and West Germany would be delighted to embrace the gold standard should the U.S., now the leading fiat money country, take the lead. But even if they do not, there is no harm done, for a gold dollar would, like the current paper dollar, be freely fluctuating in relation to other fiat paper currencies. A gold standard in the U.S. alone need provide no international monetary shock to other nations.

In addition, it is often said that we cannot go back to gold unless we first adopt monetary and fiscal stability, but if we can do that, why bother about gold?

The answer is that governments need a leash, a tight rein, in order to cease their counterfeiting and inflationary activities. The same argument, after all, could be used against a bill of rights, a constitution, or any other restraint on government. The point is that we always need a checkrein on government, in all areas. In the monetary area, the best checkrein is one wielded not by government itself but by the people themselves through being able to redeem their dollars whenever they wish in gold coin.

This does not mean that gold is a panacea for all our ills, and we must avoid the danger of overselling gold and thereby raising false hopes that would soon be dashed. Gold would not be an instant cure or quick fix for recession, sluggish growth, or high interest rates. It is indispensable for checking inflation, but the Fed could still inflate or mismanage in the short run even under the gold standard if it is determined to do so. But not for long, for it would be subjected to gold discipline, which it would have to heed. Eventually, as I have noted, we should consider liquidating the Federal Reserve System and returning to a world of unmanaged free banking under the gold standard. Short of that, I would like to see, in addition to the gold standard, a law preventing the Fed from purchasing any further assets (that are not gold), and thereby stopping the continual creation of new reserves for the commercial banks.

But I would urge that if a gold standard is adopted, it be a genuine gold standard—one where the public can redeem their dollars at will at a fixed weight in gold. While even such a gold standard would not be a panacea, it is indispensable for ending inflation and returning to sound money. Anything else would be merely a sham, and would only wrap the prestige of gold around a program of permanent inflation. Such a hoax is bound to fail; it would be worse than nothing, because then the gold standard would be unfairly discredited along with the ever shrinking dollar. The American public deserves a gold standard in reality, and not just in name.

ADDITIONAL INFORMATION

All of the special interest groups in this country have lobbyists in Washington. Fortunately, there are also nonprofit organizations engaged in education and lobbying efforts to *end* special interest legislation. For more information, you can write to:

> The American Economic Council
> 9595 Wilshire Boulevard, Suite 200
> Beverly Hills, California 90212
>
> The Mises Institute
> 325 Pennsylvania Avenue, S.E.
> Washington, D.C. 20003.

RECOMMENDED READING

SIMPLE, INTRODUCTORY MATERIAL

Bastiat, Frederic. *The Law*. Translated from the French by
Dean Russell. Irvington-on-Hudson, New York: Foundation for
Economic Education, 1950.

Bladen, Ashby. *How to Cope with the Developing Financial Crisis*.
New York: McGraw-Hill, 1980.

Bolles, Richard Nelson. *What Color is Your Parachute?
A Practical Manual for Job-Hunters and Career Changers*.
Berkeley, California: Ten Speed Press, 1972.

Browne, Harry and Coxon, Terry. *Inflation-Proofing Your Investments*.
New York: William Morrow, 1981.

The Constitution of the United States of America, 1787.

Emerson, Ralph Waldo. "Wealth." In *The Selected Writings of
Ralph Waldo Emerson*. New York: Modern Library, 1940 [1860].

Friedman, Milton and Friedman, Rose A. *Free to Choose*.
New York: Harcourt Brace Jovanovich, 1979.

Gilder, George. *Wealth and Poverty*. New York: Basic Books, 1981.

Greaves, Percy L., Jr. *Understanding the Dollar Crisis*.
Belmont, Massachusetts: Western Islands, 1973.

Hazlitt, Henry. *Economics in One Lesson*.
New Rochelle, New York: Arlington House, 1979 [1946].

Hazlitt, Henry. *What You Should Know about Inflation*.
New York: Funk and Wagnalls, 1968 [1960].

Katz, Howard S. *The Paper Aristocracy*. New York:
Books in Focus, 1976.

Lakein, Alan. *How to Get Control of Your Time and Your Life*.
New York: David McKay, 1973.

McDonald, Lawrence Patton. *We Hold These Truths*.
Seal Beach, California: '76 Press, 1976.

Mises, Ludwig von. *The Anti-Capitalistic Mentality*.
South Holland, Illinois: Libertarian Press, 1972 [1956].

Mises, Ludwig von. *Economic Policy: Thoughts for Today and Tomorrow.* South Bend, Indiana: Regnery/Gateway, 1979.

Mises, Ludwig von. *Planning for Freedom, and Sixteen Other Essays and Addresses.* South Holland, Illinois: Libertarian Press, 1952.

North, Gary. *Successful Investing in an Age of Envy.* Fort Worth, Texas: Steadman Press, 1982.

Paul, Ron. *Gold, Peace and Prosperity: The Birth of a New Currency.* Lake Jackson, Texas: The Foundation for Rational Economics and Education, 1981.

Pugsley, John A. *The Alpha Strategy.* Los Angeles: Stratford Press, 1981.

Pugsley, John A. *Common Sense Economics.* Costa Mesa, California: Common Sense Press, 1976.

Ringer, Robert J. *Restoring the American Dream.* New York: Fawcett Crest, 1979.

Rothbard, Murray N. *What Has Government Done to Our Money?* Novato, California: Libertarian Publishers, 1964.

Ruff, Howard J. *How to Prosper During the Coming Bad Years.* New York: Times Books, 1979.

Ruff, Howard J. *Survive and Win in the Inflationary Eighties.* New York: Times Books, 1981.

Simon, William E. *A Time for Truth.* New York: Reader's Digest, 1978.

Sinclair, James E. and Schulz, Harry D. *How You Can Profit from Gold.* Westport, Connecticut: Arlington House, 1980.

Smith, Jerome F. *The Coming Currency Collapse.* New York: Books in Focus, 1980.

Sutton, Anthony C. *The War on Gold.* Seal Beach, California: '76 Press, 1977.

White, Andrew Dickson. *Fiat Money Inflation in France.* Caldwell, Idaho: The Caxton Printers, 1978 [1914].

Williams, Walter E. *The State Against Blacks.* New York, McGraw-Hill, 1982.

MEDIUM COMPLEXITY

Hamilton, Alexander; Madison, James; and Jay, John.
The Federalist Papers. New York: Mentor, 1961 [1788].

Hayek, Friedrich A. *The Road to Serfdom.* Chicago:
University of Chicago Press, 1944.

Paul, Ron and Lehrman, Lewis. *The Case for Gold: A Minority
Report of the U.S. Gold Commission.* Washington, D.C.: Cato
Institute, 1982.

Rothbard, Murray N. *America's Great Depression.*
Princeton, New Jersey: D. Van Nostrand, 1963.

Rothbard, Murray N. *For a New Liberty.* New York: Macmillan, 1973.

Rothbard, Murray. *The Mystery of Banking.*
New York: Richardson and Snyder, 1983.

Sennholz, Hans F. *Age of Inflation.* Belmont, Massachusetts:
Western Islands, 1979.

Smith, Page. *The Constitution: A Documentary and Narrative
History.* New York: Morrow, 1978.

DETAILED, TECHNICAL BOOKS

Anderson, Benjamin M. *Economics and the Public Welfare:*
A Financial and Economic History of the United States, 1914–1946.
Indianapolis: Liberty Press, 1979 [1949].

Hayek, Friedrich A. *The Constitution of Liberty.*
Chicago: University of Chicago Press, 1960.

Hayek, Friedrich A. *Law, Legislation and Liberty: The Mirage*
of Social Justice. Chicago: University of Chicago Press, 1976.

Mises, Ludwig von. *Human Action: A Treatise on Economics.*
Chicago: Henry Regnery, 1966 [1949].

Mises, Ludwig von. *Liberalism: A Socio-Economic Exposition.*
Translated from the German by Ralph Raico. Kansas City:
Sheed, Andrews and McMee, 1976 [1927].

Mises, Ludwig von. *The Theory of Money and Credit.* Translated
from the German by H.E. Batson. Irvington-on-Hudson, New York:
Foundation for Economic Education, 1971 [1912].

For additional books, contact
your local bookstore or write:
    Communications Research
    P.O. Box 11143
    Oakland, CA 94611
    (415) 339-3550